seven secrets of spontaneous storytelling

Danyah Miller

Illustrated by Kate Bunce

Hawthorn Press

Hawthorn Press

Published by Hawthorn Press, Hawthorn House,
1 Lansdown Lane, Stroud, Gloucestershire, GL5 1BJ, UK
Tel: (01453) 757040   Email: info@hawthornpress.com
Website: www.hawthornpress.com

Cover design and illustrations © Kate Bunce
Typesetting by Lucy Guenot
Printed by Henry Ling Ltd, The Dorset Press, Dorchester
Printed on environmentally friendly chlorine-free paper sourced from renewable forest stock.

British Library Cataloguing in Publication Data applied for

ISBN 978-1-912480-86-9

Dedication

For Luke and Sofie,
who spur me on to become a kinder mum
and a wiser woman.

And for families everywhere,
may you be inspired to share stories
and storytelling together, always.

Contents

Slovenian Vocabulary

Babica pronounced *ba-bee-tsah* = Grandmother

Draga Moja (F) pronounced *dra-ga moya* = My Dear/
Sweetheart

Dragi Moj (M) pronounced *dra-gee moy* = My Dear/
Sweetheart

Ljubček moj (M) pronounced l*yoob-chek moy* = My
Sweetheart

Ljubica Moja (F) pronounced *lyoo-bee-tsa moya* = My
Sweetheart

Ljubim te pronounced *lyoo-bim tay* = I love you

Marija Character name, pronounced *Maria*

Moji Dragi pronounced *moyee dra-gee* = My Dears/
Sweetheart

Oprosti pronounced *o-pross-ee* = I'm Sorry

Sonček Moj pronounced *sonn-chek moy* = My Sunshine

Vrtača pronounced *vurr-tah-chah* = Sinkhole (a depres-
sion or hole in the ground caused by some form of
collapse of the surface layer)

Foreword

Here in this unique book is the inside story of a supreme storyteller. Here you can discover how the magic of storytelling is made, encouraging families everywhere to tell more stories.

I am myself a storyteller first and a writer second. But when I perform, I read the words I've written, which I love to do. But when you read you focus on the words, live the story as well as you can while reading, but always relating to the words in front of you, the turning of the pages, and that to a degree always distances you from an audience. You feel inhibited by the way you are telling it. You flow the story as best you can, but what you really want is not just to read it but to tell it as you are living it in your mind's eye, to lose yourself in the story, and take the audience by the hand and take them on the journey with you.

See Danyah in full flow on stage, and you never look away. And it's not just the staging and the lighting or the extraordinary inventiveness of puppets and props, it's the sheer intensity of her storytelling, how she moves with the story, telling it with her whole body. She invites her audience to join her in the story, and seven years of age or seventy, we go with her.

I must have read my story of *I Believe in Unicorns*, telling it as best I could, a hundred times. And until I saw Danyah performing it at festivals, in schools, in concert halls, in theatres, I thought I'd read it quite well. Never have I seen audiences more deeply engaged, tearful, joyful, rapt as when she performed it.

This book is telling us all, you can do this story-telling, you don't need the prop of a book. Tell a story as they were told of old, dance it, sing it, live it. Do it with total commitment and they'll go with you. Mean it, with your voice, your eyes, your whole being. Tell it true, eye to eye.

Do read the book, using the story and the story games to enjoy the magic of spontaneous storytelling in your own family, and, if you want a master class, go to see her, be transported.

Michael Morpurgo

Introduction

Everyone tells stories. Although most people would not consider themselves to be 'storytellers', we all are. Humans are storytelling-beings. You and I are storytellers, whether we recognise it or not. We share anecdotes and memories, tell jokes, describe experiences, spin yarns. Our lives are made up of stories. We listen to songs, are persuaded by adverts, read books, listen to the radio, understand our history through the stories of those who came before us, watch films and TV.

We make sense of the world through story. Stories feed us to our very core.

What I love so much about spontaneous storytelling is that anyone can do it, anywhere and with any number of people. You don't need to be an expert storyteller, have a good memory, or even have time to prepare. All you need to do is to be present, then listen, let go and have fun. Stories told off-the-cuff offer us a door into infinite adventures, a special playground where we can be and do anything that our imagination can conjure – and as we take off into this world, we can carry our listeners with us.

I wrote this book to share the seven secrets of spontaneous storytelling, so that you can become a confident storyteller and have fun playing story games with your family and friends. There are few pleasures children love more than hearing their parents telling them stories.

The seeds of this book were sown many years ago when I was a young child. I played around a neglected, bricked up windmill close to my parents' home in York and around a tumbled down cottage in the Yorkshire Dales during the holidays. I spent days cloud watching, inventing stories in my imagination and collecting treasures – a stone, twig or piece of sheep's wool – for my father to turn into a tale around the open fire. My dad kept these items in a beautiful, small oak box that he had made, and would ask me to choose one to use as a springboard into a tall tale. He always began his stories, 'Once upon a time... '

I don't remember the content of these made-up stories, but I remember how they made me feel. This time together with my father made me laugh, think, question, be curious and feel loved.

I forgot all about my father's improvised tales until many years later when I was introduced to spontaneous storytelling in my work. I realised that this storytelling genre is akin to devising theatre, always my favourite form of theatre since college days. This ancient art, stretching back to Roman times, is used for television and radio programmes such as *Whose Line is it Anyway?*, *Would I Lie to You?* and *Just a Minute*, which all rely heavily on improvisation and spontaneity.

It seems to me that flexibility and adaptability are key skills for us to cultivate as we live through extraordinary changes in the world. Unlike during my childhood, there are far greater challenges and demands on parents today, not least that we are constantly bombarded with ways to entertain our children, to keep them busy and occupied.

As a step-parent and parent I often struggled to find creative and empowering solutions to the many trials we faced as a family. On reflection, it was stories and storytelling which helped me most to navigate some of the stormiest of times.

When my young stepson came to stay, he would wake several times in the night, crying and miserable, until I came up with the idea of building him a den. Together we upturned the sofa and chairs and covered them with blankets before filling the space with pillows and a duvet. He loved it. From then on bedtime was an adventure. Each night I told him a story as he drifted into sleep, cocooned and safe.

My daughter was a feisty, challenging child. I often used stories, games, play and humour when she kicked and screamed, refusing to co-operate, or when she was frustrated, tired or hungry. On my best days, we lay on the trampoline sharing cloud stories when she needed quiet time and I told stories when she was feeling anxious. Her friends asked me to play story games when I drove them home. Jumping on a magical carpet of stories was the only way I could get her to walk up the very steep hill to school. I certainly didn't always get it right, but these storytelling games were immensely helpful to me, averting at least some of the crises! This book is an opportunity for you to share these family tested storytelling tools for yourself.

Many years later, in my solo, theatrical storytelling show *I Believe in Unicorns*, adapted from the story by Michael Morpurgo, we include a spontaneous story which I share with audiences at the point when eight-year-old Tomas, who hates reading and school, meets the librarian in his local library. At each performance I ask members of the audience to call out a Name, a Place and an Object. I then weave these into a three-minute story, whilst being timed. It has been incredible, hilarious and at times terrifying, to open my heart to allow a spontaneous story to flow through me, using only these random words and my imagination.

My decision, therefore, to write this book in the form of a tale about a young family exploring storytelling was an easy one, not least because I have witnessed the incredible power of story. I know from experience how much fun story games are when we play together. I also know that stories considerably help us to digest and remember what we've learnt.

The purpose of this book is to share the secrets of storytelling that I have learnt from being a parent, from working with families, with children in schools, in theatres and from so many wise women in my life. I would like to pass these secrets on to you now. I hope they will inspire you and give you the confidence to become a storytelling family, so that you can benefit from the deep nourishment of stories for many years to come.

Here you will find ideas, story games and provocations to help you easily create tales 'out of the air' with and for your families and friends. The tools, tips and tricks in the book are simple and fun, designed for you to follow, adapt and add to, to fit your own particular circumstances. They can be shared with large and small groups of children in a school, library, outside or in your home.

Each Secret has its own chapter, which is explored through the lens of the troubled Dale family:

1. A Welcome Stranger: *The First Secret – Imagination*
2. Is She For Real?: *The Second Secret – Observation and Senses*

Each chapter has a games section for easy reference.

The Dales, like many families, encounter difficulties as they navigate the day-to-day challenges of life with their three children. Darinka and Adam Dale are looking for help. This support comes to them in the form of a Wise Woman, Dorothy, who appears unexpectedly one day seemingly from nowhere.

I offer this book to you, with love...

Danyah Miller

The Ups and Downs of the Dales

If there is light in the soul,
there will be beauty in the person.
If there is beauty in the person,
there will be harmony in the house.
If there is harmony in the house,
there will be order in the nation.
If there is order in the nation,
there will be peace in the world.'
Chinese Proverb

Adam Dale was certainly not a natural father. He loved his job as a builder and carpenter, particularly because it was physically strenuous and demanding. He left early each morning and didn't finish work until the sun was setting, after which he was often persuaded by his mates to join them for a pint. This left little time for his six-year-old son, Tommy, and his three-year-old twins, Marija and Luka.

It was a balmy August evening; a cool breeze soothed his face after an intense and hot week. Adam promised himself he would be back in time to put Tommy to bed. But with his second beer set in front of him by Si, his best mate since childhood, he washed away the image of Tommy sucking his thumb in his tiny, darkened bedroom.

'Come on mate, you deserve it,' Si encouraged Adam. 'It's been a helluva week.' Si also had a family, but since he only came to the pub on a Friday night Adam justified being there to catch up with him.

It wasn't that Adam didn't love his kids – or at least that's what he told himself. He just didn't know how to connect with them. He was bewildered by their constant and seemingly boundless energy and his temper flared quickly at Tommy's demands, questions and tears.

By the time Adam walked up the hill to their terraced cottage, sheepishly opening the lime green front door, he was certain they would be deeply asleep. From one day to the next he was less sure about the greeting he would receive from his partner, Darinka.

'Tommy asked for you tonight,' she said stonily, without looking at him. 'You promised to be home to read *Bear Hunt* to him. Why didn't you come home?'

Adam hung his head. He stayed silent, wanting to ward off the inevitable argument.

'Adam, why?' demanded Darinka. 'This is the third time this week.'

He dropped his sweater on the sofa, unlaced his boots and headed to the kitchen to pour himself a juice. Darinka followed, goading him.

'Don't you want to come home? What's so bad about being here?'

Darinka was furious. 'You have to come home and help me.'

Adam looked away, unable to meet Darinka's gaze. 'Sorry Dinks,' he said quietly, the words sticking in his throat. He wanted to explain that it had been a stressful week on site. They had missed deadlines, which would result in penalties, and he was worried about money, but he also knew that going to the pub after work was not a good enough reason to let Darinka down. Internally, he swore to make it up to her over the weekend.

Darinka wouldn't let it drop. She followed him from room to room, trying to get him to speak to her. 'You know holidays are tough for me, it's exhausting. I'm exhausted,' she said, her words trailing off.

Sighing heavily, she resigned herself to the fact that when Adam was confronted, he shut down. She resented that she had to be patient and wait for him to open up, which happened so rarely these days. She locked and bolted the front door, folded his sweater and put his boots in the small utility area behind the kitchen. Adam would clean them tomorrow, ready for work.

As she climbed the stairs to their bedroom, Darinka thought about the two whole weeks ahead of her before Tommy returned to school and the twins started nursery a couple of days a week. She wanted to pack her bags now and run away, back home to dissolve into her mother's arms.

But for Darinka, going home wasn't as simple as walking down the road. Adam was surrounded by aunts and uncles, cousins and friends. She'd been born and raised into a large, boisterous family in Slovenia, but here she felt alone.

As Darinka lay in bed, unable to sleep, she thought back

to the first time she had met Adam, 13 years ago. She was finishing her final school exams, whilst 19-year-old Adam was backpacking his way across Europe with Si and two other mates. As she and her friends were sitting in Kavarna Rog, Darinka's favourite cafe in central Ljubljana, the noisy Brits had burst in, causing quite a stir.

They were due to fly home from Croatia and wanted to make the most of their final two days. Si dared Adam to approach the girls and offer to buy them a drink, he being the most charming of the group!

Darinka had giggled, her heart beating fast, as she stared into his soft brown eyes.

Although her spoken English was basic, they managed to introduce themselves before she and her friends made space for the guys. As Adam sat opposite Darinka he blushed, feeling suddenly coy. She learnt later that he'd told his friends he'd never met such a beautiful girl. She had seemed smart and confident while he felt awkward and clumsy.

This first meeting had been brief, their conversation broken and clumsy, yet Adam and Darinka were instantly intoxicated by one another. The next day she had even driven him fifty minutes to Gabrovka to show him where she lived. They chatted and laughed all day. When she dropped him back at the bus station in Ljubljana to board the bus heading for Split airport she said, touching his arm gently, 'I don't want you to go.'

'Come with me then,' he'd responded impulsively, half meaning it. Adam texted her as soon as he landed.

She had responded before the double ticks had turned blue.

Darinka was so smitten that after several heated arguments with her parents, she had switched her university place from law to the faculty of arts to study English.

Adam could not stop thinking about her. He called and texted her daily and sent flowers and cards on a regular basis. He took time off work whenever he could, but with no direct flights from Leeds to Slovenia it was complicated to see each other. So, when Darinka completed her degree, he immediately paid for her to have an extended holiday in his home village.

'I want you to stay with me, always,' he'd told her many times. 'My friends and family love you. Si and Shuba think you're the best. Your English is brilliant.'

When she fell pregnant with Tommy, not long afterwards, they were certain they wanted to be together, but Adam was blunt. 'You know my work's here, don't you? I won't find work in Slovenia, I can't speak the language.'

She had known Adam would never leave his home and move to Slovenia but at the time she thought it didn't matter because she was excited to travel and spread her wings.

As she drifted off to sleep, thoughts of this early time and frustration about the current situation mingled together.

Adam watched a film well into the night, intentionally waiting until Darinka was asleep before he slipped into bed. Since the twins had been born, coming up for four years ago, there was a constant tension inside him. He was angry with himself for being unable to change old habits, which were clearly pushing Darinka away, but he was also furious with the children for being a source of conflict between them. Now, in the darkness, he secretly admitted to himself that he wished he hadn't had children at all. It was too much responsibility. In the early days they were carefree: they had gone away with Shubu and Si, had reckless parties, stayed out all night, joked around and shared secrets. He loved her deeply, but recently she had become so serious and was always cross with him. There was no time for the two of them. The kids came first. Tomorrow will be different, he promised himself, as he too fell asleep.

Tommy ran into their room at first light and jumped onto the bed next to his dad. Adam pulled the duvet over his head in an attempt to stave off the barrage of noise. Marija and Luka were close behind. Darinka sat up, yawning, helping them up. It was a little after 5.30am.

'Good morning, *moji dragi*. What shall we do today?'

The wind rattled the bedroom windows. A summer storm was brewing. Deep, heavy clouds were building across the sky, casting dark shadows into the room. She had planned to take the kids for a walk along the canal towpath that ran behind their row of houses. She would have to revise this plan.

'Dada, Dada, play!' Tommy climbed up onto the mound of Adam. His son was laughing and trying to pull the covers away. Adam held tighter to them. For Tommy this was the best game ever. His determined squeals of joy delighted Marija who joined in, rolling onto her back and kicking her legs in the air. Adam just wanted to sleep.

'Shh, *moji dragi*,' their mum repeated, conscious that their neighbours in the adjoining terrace would still be asleep.

'Adam?' Darinka whispered, 'let Tommy under the covers.'

Adam resisted again.

After a while Darinka couldn't bear it anymore. 'Come on you guys, let's go and feed Nala and make some breakfast.' She pulled Tommy gently away from Adam's form.

'I'll make some for you, Dada,' Luka called as they headed out of the bedroom.

'Me too,' said Tommy.

Marija was making her way downstairs, calling for the cat.

Darinka's heart hurt to see the children desperate for their father's attention and not receiving it.

By the time Adam appeared, over three hours later, the toys, crayons, Playdoh and jigsaw pieces were strewn across the sitting room floor. He appreciated that Darinka had kept the kids occupied so he could sleep longer. She was at the table colouring with Luka whilst Marija and Tommy were on the floor close by, building a Duplo castle.

Adam's presence immediately changed the dynamic. Tommy jumped up, knocking over the castle turret, causing Marija to scream.

'Stop being a cry baby!' Tommy shouted severely, swiping at his sister.

'I'm not crying,' said Marija, curling into a tiny ball, hiding her head in her arms.

'Dada, come and look at what I've made.'

'Don't hit your sister,' shouted Adam, not looking at Tommy but walking straight past him towards the kitchen.'D'ya want a coffee, Dinks?'

'Have a look at the incredible castle, Tommy and Marija...' she breathed deeply, the strain of their many unfinished arguments rising in her.

The children's noise escalated. Tommy pushed Luka away as his young brother tried to add building blocks to the tower. Marija began to cry again as her mum gently picked her up and carried her over to the sofa. Luka bit Tommy on the leg as Adam, coffee in hand, walked back into the sitting room. Tommy screamed. Adam shouted at Tommy again. 'Don't hit your brother.'

His next sudden announcement cut through the noise: 'I'm going down to the site to check the tarpaulins. This wind's fierce and I'm not sure they're tied off securely enough. I'll be back later.' The children were suddenly silent as Adam downed his coffee, and slammed his mug on the table.

'Please don't, Adam.' Darinka put Marija down onto the sofa as she stood to move towards him, trying to put her arms round his waist.

She whispered so the children wouldn't hear, 'Let Si or one of the others go – please.'

But as he removed her arms from him, his eyes steely, her voice rose. 'Not again! I need your help. It's not fair. Play with the children. It's Saturday.'

Darinka called after him as he went to collect his boots. 'You're always at work!'

Adam couldn't bear the constant crying and

screaming, but he also couldn't bear Darinka's pleading and his inability to respond to it. He walked back into the sitting room, face flushed.

'What d'ya mean it isn't fair? I've got a job to do. I told you, I won't be long.' His jaw clenched; a pulse throbbed in his forehead.

'You always say that, but I don't believe you. You've got a job here too, but you're never here. I'm sick of it.' Darinka stared at him, sick of the repetition of this argument. Adam ignored Tommy pulling at his hand.

'Dada, don't go. I'll show you my tower and you can see the knights,' Tommy begged, standing between his parents. He'd witnessed their arguments many times. 'Dada, don't go,' he continued. 'Let Uncle Si go. Dada, play with me.' When Adam continued to ignore his plea, Tommy stamped his foot, 'You never play with me! You're always at work!'

'Don't tell me what to do!' Adam's temper flared, hearing Tommy repeat his mother's words. He pulled his hand away from his son. 'Go to your room now. You're giving me a headache.' Tommy tripped backwards and fell on Marija.

'It's not fair, you're never here,' screamed Tommy as he punched out at his father.

Adam grabbed his son and shook him. 'Don't you ever speak to me like that again.'

Darinka rushed forwards to protect Tommy. Adam was reeling, unable to calm himself down. Darinka knelt beside Tommy, gathering him into her arms and calling out to Adam, 'Go. I don't care. Look what you've done. Go away.' She turned her back on Adam as she stroked the hair away from her son's tear-stained eyes, '*Ljubček moj*, it's okay, let's go and feed the ducks. Where's your hat?'

Adam was incensed. He grabbed his coat and slammed the door behind him, his son's howls ringing in his ears. He strode down the middle of the road, fighting the wind, fighting his emotions, his own stupidity and his own righteous indignation.

CHAPTER I

A Welcome Stranger
The First Secret – Imagination

'Logic will get you from A to B.
Imagination will take you everywhere.'
Albert Einstein

Darinka was breathing heavily as she gathered up her thoughts and the three children simultaneously, sitting them down for a silent and sullen breakfast, before announcing:

'Get your shoes and coats on now. We're going to the canal.'

'Can we go into the woods, Mama?' Marija asked, as she pulled on her pumps.

Darinka didn't speak. Her whole body was tense. She felt like an empty shell, serving everyone except herself. Who was she anymore? She wanted to scream, to leave this whole mess behind, but she didn't have that option like he did. The children, afraid of her temper, got ready quickly and waited by the front door. Darinka closed her eyes, breathing deeply to compose herself.

The rain hadn't amounted to more than a summer shower and the clouds were beginning to break up, however the wind was fierce. The children hid behind their mum, using her as a shield as they walked up past four of the neighbours' terraces, towards a break in the houses where a narrow snicket led down a flight of steps to the canal path.

They turned right towards the bridge, on the other side of which was a stile that led into the fields. Darinka decided that Marija's suggestion to go to the woods at the top of Tupp Hill was a good one. They could play hide and seek and this would give her a moment to catch her breath. During this holiday they had already walked along the towpath regularly, but nonetheless Darinka called out crossly when the children raced ahead.

'Come back here to me now. It's not safe to run in this wind.'

Once they were over the stile, with two fields distance between her and home, Darinka inhaled deeply, breathing out through her mouth, her shoulders dropping noticeably. The wind was scattering the clouds, revealing a deep blue sky. A flock of geese screeched overhead, disrupting the children's game of tag and shocking Tommy into tears again. He ran back to his mum and Luka joined in with his brother's wails. He pushed Tommy out of the way in order to get closer to their mum. Darinka knelt down to reassure them both. She was cross with herself for shouting at Adam in front of them, but angrier with him for provoking her. It was such a vicious circle and she didn't know how to stop it happening.

She looked up and smiled to see her fiery young

daughter striding ahead, oblivious of the storm raging around her. 'Come on you two, see how far ahead Marija's got. Can you all race up to the mill together?' she asked.

Tommy didn't need a second prompt. He ran as fast as he could, pushing Luka aside to take the lead.

'Take Luka with you, *ljubček moj*,' their mum shouted. 'Don't go beyond the mill.'

She watched them catch up with Marija, the three racing with all their might. She called out again, 'Not beyond, do you hear?' It made her chuckle that Marija could already outwit and often outrun her two brothers.

Darinka continued to walk slowly up Tupp Hill, towards the old disused windmill at the top where she knew the children would wait for her. Adam had played around this same spot as a boy. He had told them many tales about breaking in through the windows, playing catch or hide-and-seek with Si and his other mates. When Darinka first arrived in England almost nine years ago, he'd taken her to lie on this hill and watch the stars. He had made her feel safe and loved in this place, so far from her home.

'You're my shining star, Dinks,' he had said to her. She breathed deeply, softened by the memory of that evening.

Beyond the mill were the woods. Ordinarily she would have made a picnic, but today she had only remembered to bring water. The children loved coming here. Darinka hoped that leaning against the crumbling mill together would be the remedy they all needed.

To her surprise, as she reached the crown of the hill she saw the door to the windmill, previously boarded over with old planks, was open, its five sails turning in the wind. She could smell an appetising aroma of soup mingled with gingerbread. She hesitated, confused that Adam hadn't mentioned any restoration of the mill, including the sails. She was sure he'd told her they were so rotten they had been taken down when he was a kid.

'An accident waiting to happen,' he'd said. She panicked and called out, 'Tommy, Marija, Luka where are you? You're not inside, are you? It's not safe.'

'Mama, we're round here, come, come,' Tommy called back.

She followed the sound of his voice. The three of them were standing close to a woman who was sitting on a bench, wrapped in a large tatty pink and orange woollen shawl. All three children were listening intently. The woman's broad and cheeky smile reminded Darinka so much of her own mother that she was rendered speechless, her mouth gaping open. Sunlight dappling across the woman's face made her appear to come from another time and place. She had grey-green dancing eyes and a gentle weather-worn face lined with age. Her reddy-grey hair was piled up in a messy knot, fastened in place with a large antique butterfly clip. Darinka took a step closer towards the bench, mesmerised by the woman, uncertain whether to reach out to shake hands or how to ask about the windmill, about which she was confused.

Before either woman had a chance to speak, Tommy grabbed his mum's hand and pointed. 'She says fairies and elves live in the meadow'.

'I'm sure they do,' chuckled Darinka. The woman

gestured for her to sit on the bench.

'Lovely to see you, pet. My name's Dorothy.' She turned to the children, 'Children usually prefer to call me Dotty – I suppose I am a bit.' She winked at them cheekily. 'What's your name, young man?'

Tommy laughed. 'That's a funny name. I'm Tomas, but everyone calls me Tommy. I'm six-and-a-half. This is Luka and my sister Marija. They're only little and I'm big. In six more sleeps they'll be four.' Tommy looked up at his mum, tugging her hand, his smile revealing that all his earlier fears had blown away. 'I'm going to look under that large tree, Mama. Dotty says we might be able to make a den there.'

Darinka nodded as Tommy and the twins bolted off to the oak tree at the edge of the wood. Although on the edge of tears, all the tension dissipated as her body relaxed, knowing the children were safe. Her thoughts flashed back to playing outside all day with her own brothers and sisters: as zookeepers, stilt-walkers or moon explorers. This unknown woman, who had effortlessly drawn the children into a magical world, made her feel so at ease. Darinka wanted to throw her arms around her, but instead she smiled and, holding out her hand awkwardly, said, 'Hello, I'm Darinka. My children seem to have already introduced themselves!'

Dorothy patted the seat, inviting Darinka to join her.

'Tommy isn't usually that chatty,' Darinka said as she made herself comfortable on the bench, kicking off her shoes and tucking her feet underneath her.

She was surprised that Tommy had gone off to

explore without her. He was usually quite a shy boy who clung to his mum when he was faced with new circumstances. His teacher had noticed that he had become more nervous. Darinka worried that it was exacerbated by the increasing number of arguments between Adam and her. She found herself telling Dorothy about the children.

'The twins are definitely more robust than their brother. Marija already organises the others. She's quite a force of nature!'

'You've got your hands full haven't you. But there's something else troubling you isn't there, pet?'

Although Darinka knew nothing about this strange woman, she seemed warm and kind. As Darinka began spilling out her daily worries and frustrations, she realised how isolated she felt and how desperately she needed help and advice. As she shared more, instinctively trusting Dorothy, she spoke about her arguments with Adam and his lack of connection to the children.

Dorothy listened, nodding once or twice but saying nothing, even when Darinka paused. This extended silence gave Darinka the space and permission to speak freely and openly. 'It all seems so petty when I speak it out loud,' she said, tears welling in her eyes, and she caught her breath. 'I'm fine, I'm fine, but sometimes when someone asks how I am, I get a bit tearful. I feel much better now, I'm fine... fine.' She wiped a tear from her cheek, laughing uncomfortably, trying to make light of it.

Dorothy smiled kindly, offering Darinka a small cotton hanky with a pink heart embroidered in one corner. She remained silent.

Darinka took the hanky, clutching it in her fist. It felt comforting. Other than Shubu, Si's partner, Darinka didn't have anyone she felt able to confide in. She stared off towards the children on the edge of the woods. It was astonishing to see them happily lost in play. She'd become so used to their demands, arguments and outbursts. She coughed and turned back towards Dorothy, her eyes now puffy with tears. 'I'm amazed by how absorbed they are,' she said. What had Dorothy said to encourage them to go off and play?

Dorothy chuckled, reading Darinka's mind. 'I told them a story about Little Gnomie Blue Hat who lives at the foot of that old oak. Like Tommy, Little Blue Hat is shy, but he loves to have the company of children as they know how to play alongside him. I told Tommy that if they worked quietly, Little Blue Hat might join them. I suggested that, if they used their bright eyes, they'd find everything they needed to build a secret den in that hollow next to the tree.'

Dorothy reminded Darinka of her favourite teacher, Miss Zorac, who was empathetic but also grounded and authentic. Dorothy had the same razor-sharp delivery as her teacher. Darinka leant forwards, asking to hear more.

'Imagination is a powerful muscle, pet. We all have it, but it weakens if we don't use it – like any muscle really. Imagination is rather magical when you think about it.' Dorothy nodded her head, touching her lips with her fingertips as she reflected, 'It's what gives us the ability to innovate, problem solve, to navigate unfamiliar situations...' She trailed off, deep in thought, before continuing. 'Storytelling strengthens our imagination. The children respond so well to stories don't they, pet?'

Darinka had not thought about stories much, other than as part of a bedtime routine and to help the children learn to read for themselves. Talking with Dorothy was making her curious to understand more.

'Why should we share stories, what makes them so important for children?'

Dorothy touched her lips again and pushed a strand of hair away from her face. Darinka's question hung in the air. 'That is such a good question, pet. I think it's one that we shouldn't answer too quickly.' She shook her head, as if wrestling with her thoughts. Darinka looked down at her hands. The left was cupping her right, as she too contemplated the question, before becoming distracted wondering who Dorothy was and how she had come to live in the Windmill.

Dorothy's words brought Darinka's attention back to the wise woman. 'It's a good question. A glib answer would be that stories are more interesting than a list of facts and figures and that they make learning easier and more fun,' Dorothy laughed. 'What do you think?'

Darinka certainly enjoyed reading to the kids, but bedtime wasn't easy and she was often exhausted by the end of a full day with them. The children fought about which book they wanted, which meant she read several books to satisfy them all. From the way other mums spoke at school she was convinced they were better at it than her. She wished Adam would come home and take on this responsibility but knew that was unlikely, she had asked him so many times.

Thoughts flicked simultaneously across her mind. How desperately she craved time to herself, how she couldn't remember exactly what it was like to go out to work or to have her evenings free, to speak her own language with friends, not to feel so isolated. She yearned for adult conversation yet felt so depleted at night. How would it change when the twins started nursery in September? As August babies they would start so young, which she felt sad about. She and her siblings hadn't started school till they were six.

Her face looked troubled again as she struggled to answer Dorothy's question.

Dorothy spoke slowly and gently, the words washing over Darinka like a soothing balm. 'Personally I believe that stories are how we make sense of the world. They're what make us human. My experience is that when we share stories with children they can nourish both them and us, on such a deep level.' Dorothy lent over and touched Darinka's hands softly. 'Don't forget that we're all storytellers, sharing stories every day with each other. You don't have to wait till bedtime pet, or even always read from a book.'

Darinka wished it were that easy, her doubts and lack of confidence were drilling into her brain, even as Dorothy carried on.

'Try weaving stories into your daily activities with the twins,' Dorothy continued. 'It'll help them to learn. When my children and grandchildren were young I found made-up stories very useful to transition from one activity to the next. One of mine hated being disturbed when she was engrossed in play, even if it was to do something else she loved. I didn't always get it right, but I found that songs and rhymes eased the process for her. I made up a short story about a lost wolf cub who asked her to lead the way. We made up lots of stories about that cub. Another time, when I was concerned that my eldest wasn't drinking enough, I created a tale about the last little dinosaur on earth who could only drink special dino-water and needed my son's help to collect it from the well.'

Dorothy laughed, pausing to wait for the sound of a plane to subside. Darinka untangled her feet and stretched out her legs, pulling at her jeans. She leant back against the bench, feeling the sun on her face, listening as Dorothy continued, 'They were simple, imperfect stories. You don't have to make finished or polished stories for children to love them, pet. In fact, in my experience, when the children see that ours are flawed, they're more likely to make up their own. It takes the pressure off them somehow and gives them confidence.'

Tommy ran up to the two women, closely followed by Marija, who threw herself into her mother's lap, before being pushed aside by Tommy.

'Where is the Little Blue Hat? We didn't see him.' Marija stared at Dotty, lips pouting and hands on her hips.

'It's 'cos you and Tommy were making too much noise,' said Luka, stabbing at Tommy.

'No, we weren't,' said Tommy, shaking his head in his brother's face.

'Yes!' replied Luka, kicking at Tommy's ankle.

Tommy ignored him, continuing his questions,

'Dotty, how do you know where he lives? Have you ever seen him?'

'Why can't we see him?' asked Luka. 'Is he shy?'

Dotty gave each of their questions serious consideration and Darinka noticed that her sentences often began with the words 'I wonder...?', drawing the children closer. Marija stroked Dorothy's soft shawl. Both she and Luka stared into the Wise Woman's eyes, their mouths open wide.

Dorothy dropped her voice to a whisper as if sharing a secret. This increased their curiosity and seemed to bring them huge pleasure. 'Little Blue Hat is quite difficult to spot you know, but I bet he's been watching as you build your den.'

They stood in awed silence, wondering, until Marija said slowly, 'I don't believe he's there.' And then adamantly, 'I didn't see him.'

Dorothy's eyes twinkled. Luka looked crest fallen.

'Maybe you're right, pet,' said Dotty softly, 'but maybe he's like the wind. We can't always see the wind, can we?'

Darinka was struck by how genuinely interested and absorbed Dorothy was in the conversation.

'See,' said Tommy triumphantly, 'he is there. He's like the wind.'

Dorothy told Darinka that she had learnt from experience how valuable it was to let young children wonder about things. Not to answer their questions too literally, so they could produce solutions for themselves, suitable both to their age of development and their natural temperament. She began to share a rhyme:

I met a little Gnome one day,
beneath the old oak tree.
I wondered why he hid away,
and would not speak to me.
He tipped his hat, with feather in,
and then he told me that,
his play was work, my work was play,
a lot more fun than chat.

As she spoke, she created clear, simple hand gestures, which sat alongside the words and depicted the tree, the gnome hiding and him raising his hat. She didn't look at the children but instead gazed towards her hands as if she could see the gnome. Even when she repeated the verse a second and third time.

Darinka was as spellbound as the children. Darinka had rarely seen her children this still before. Marija hardly sat for a moment – Adam called her his 'little firecracker'. Dorothy must be a child whisperer, Darinka thought to herself.

'Let's go and find Little Blue Hat,' Marija murmured to her brothers, imitating Dorothy's quiet tone. They tiptoed off, holding hands, back towards the tree, whispering to each other.

As soon as the children left, Darinka moved closer to Dorothy, asking how it was that the children were prepared to listen so keenly to the same song, three times.

Dorothy thought for a moment then replied, 'The more vividly you picture the world of the song or story the more they're able to see Little Blue Hat in their imaginations. Children can easily live both in their imaginations and in what we call reality.' She paused before continuing brightly, 'I learnt an interesting fact recently. Apparently, we humans find pleasure in groups of threes. Our brains are always looking for patterns and three is the minimum number needed to make one. So, evidently, when we subconsciously spot a pattern it makes us feel safe.' Dorothy let out an uninhibited laugh, full of delight, slapping her hands onto her knees in pure joy. 'I find that fascinating. It puts some proper science behind what I was doing instinctively!'

Darinka was beginning to appreciate the deep wisdom being shared with her.

'Repetition is how children learn language,' Dorothy continued, 'of course, it also helps them to relax, which makes them more receptive to learning. I've often told the same story for many days or even over weeks without children tiring of it.'

Darinka snorted. Repositioning her feet, which were numb from sitting on them, she explained how frustrated Adam got when the children begged for the same book again and again.

'Oh, yes, pet, we adults... we get very bored with this repetition, don't we? But it's so valuable for children. Maybe suggest to Adam that he makes up a story about a family who can have different adventures throughout the year. That way he gets to enjoy the changes, while the children enjoy the repetition and familiarity of stories surrounding one family.'

Darinka wasn't sure Adam would know where to start, but she was completely fascinated by what Dorothy was telling her.

'If Adam were to make up stories for them, they'd

learn so much about the seasons from him. He's out in all weathers isn't he, pet? We're so lucky to have such varied seasons in this country. Although he might not agree with us when his hands are freezing cold and he's soaking wet!'

Darinka had so many questions for Dorothy and wished that Adam could hear her too. Her thoughts were racing as she ran her hand through her hair and breathed in sharply, picking up a whiff of the sweet gingerbread.

'What a gift it is for children when teachers use stories across all the subjects. You can do the same at home, pet. Whatever you're doing with the children, whether it's cooking, tidying up, getting them to brush their teeth...

'My first grandchild, Noah, hated having his long, curly hair brushed. He would scream and kick and do anything he could to stop his mum. One night when he was staying with me, I told him a story, which I made up, about a little girl who found a golden comb in the mountains belonging to the bears. She wanted to take it home and the bears agreed if she promised to bring it back. At home her mum combed her curly, golden locks until they were silky smooth. I don't remember the exact story but the amazing thing about it was that Noah never complained about us brushing his hair again. We always referred to his hair as his golden locks. A rich image for a child to enjoy.'

She paused in reflection and then chuckled. 'That was a long time ago. He has two of his own children now!'

It seemed so simple when Dorothy spoke, but Darinka's head was bursting with thoughts about how she could make up stories.

Dorothy continued, 'Using stories in this way is wonderful to help children process what's happening to them and to connect to their surroundings.'

Marija raced back towards them as Dorothy was speaking. The wise woman could only see her out of the corner of her eye, but she extended her arm towards the child in a welcoming gesture. Marija, held in her embrace, didn't interrupt until Dorothy had finished her conversation. Then she turned to Marija, 'Now, pet, thank you for being patient. Tell me, what treasures have you found?'

Marija was beaming as she shared details about the worms and a snail she had found. Tommy and Luka joined them.

'The den's nearly ready!' said Tommy with pride.

'You look at it, come...' Luka pulled at Dorothy's blue velvet skirt.

Dorothy stood. As she arched her back and stretched her arms wide, she groaned loudly. 'Well now, these old bones aren't what they used to be and here I am prattling on for so long.' The sun warmed her back and the breeze blew strands of hair across her face. 'I'd love to see what you've made.' The children shrieked in glee as she swept the strands of hair away. The twins raced ahead, pulling Dorothy whilst Tommy led his mum by the hand, earnestly explaining what they had been building. Darinka was amused to hear Adam's voice so clearly in that of her son.

When eventually they returned to the bench Dorothy lowered herself down to kneel next to a little patch of earth. She patted the grass next to her, indicating for the children to sit. All three of them dropped instantly into a circle around her. Darinka joined them.

'Let's play a game.' Dorothy absentmindedly pulled out a weed from the tiny garden.

'Mama, Mama let's play, let's play,' the children squealed.

Darinka grinned, love flooding through her. It was the simplest of things that made her children most content.

'So,' said Dorothy, 'the ABC game. I'll begin. My first sentence will start with a word beginning with the letter A. Then I'll pass the story to your mama to continue and her sentence will begin with the letter B. Tommy will you be able to continue the story from your mama using the letter C to form the first word in your sentence?'

'Of course,' said Tommy, snuggling closer to Dotty and smiling up into her face.

Dorothy began, 'Although it was a chilly day, Anna was out in the garden planting and weeding.'

She looked across at Darinka, who hesitated, panicked for a moment but then, glancing around for inspiration from what she saw, said, 'Buttercups and daisies were scattered across the grass and Anna wondered whether or not to pull them up or leave them be.'

The twins giggled. Tommy was thinking hard, anxious to get it right. He put his hand in front of his mouth and looked around, muttering words to himself, 'Can't decide.'

'This game should always be filled with joy rather than rules!' Dotty whispered to Darinka, winking at her, before turning to Tommy. 'Very clever, pet.'

Tommy smiled coyly, more confident now he'd made Dotty and his mum laugh. He continued the story, 'Can't decide... I'm going to ask my mate Carl. Anna ran to find him sitting in a tree.' The twins wanted to join in, so Dorothy looked across at Luka and whispered,'D.'

'Dotty, Little Blue Hat and me is having jam sandwiches. Your turn, Marija'.

Marija was uncharacteristically silent. She moved closer to Dotty, staring at the woman.

Dotty put her arm around Marija reassuringly, whispering, 'Shall I give you a suggestion?'

Marija nodded, dropping her eyes to the ground.

Tommy called out several words, 'Eating, even, Edward, everything.'

'Those are great words... What do you reckon?' asked Dorothy quietly.

'What about everyone?' Darinka suggested.

'Everyone have jam sandwiches with Little Blue Hat.' Marija blurted out quickly. Her brothers clapped and cheered and she beamed.

The story took crazy twists and turns. When one or other of them was stuck, their siblings dived in to help. Dorothy wove previous parts of the story back into the narrative, much to everyone's delight. She made it clear to Darinka that it didn't matter if someone hadn't started the sentence with the correct letter. There was lots of laughter and made-up words as they came to X, Y and Z.

'They picked that game up quickly, didn't they? I thought the twins would struggle, they're only little!'

Dorothy said, as she leant forward to push herself up from the ground.

Darinka smiled widely. 'I'm so impressed with the game, we'll definitely be playing it again won't we kids?'

Luka whispered to his mum, 'I'm hungry Mama.'

'I'm so cross, I only brought water. I'm not sure how I'll get Luka home without a tantrum,' Darinka confided in Dorothy.

'It's time for our own picnic isn't it?' Dorothy said, winking at Luka as she smoothed down her skirt and tidied her shawl around her.

Darinka smiled at Dorothy. 'Thank you,' she mouthed.

'Before I go to prepare it,' Dorothy beckoned the children towards her, 'I'd like your help. Could you scamper off, like little mice and find me something yellow, something green and something brown?' As they stood up, ready to scurry, Dorothy touched her lips with one of her fingers before confiding in them that little mice were always gentle with Mother Earth and would never snatch anything that was growing.

'Eek, eek,' Tommy said quietly, nodding assent.

'Eek, eek,' Marija and Luka copied.

'When you're back the picnic will be ready.'

Dorothy glanced at Darinka who'd sat back on the bench, eyes closed, face tilted towards the sun. The door banged behind Dorothy but she reappeared moments later carrying a tray laden with soup, jam sandwiches, slices of cucumber, carrots and celery, small apples, gingerbread and a pot of freshly picked mint tea.

'I don't know how you get them to play so easily,' said Darinka, as she helped to spread out a flowery cloth for the food.

'Ah, but you see, children are born with enormous amounts of creativity and resourcefulness. Small children left to their own devices can be endlessly inventive. We can help them by nurturing their natural abilities. Playing story games and creating stories are a wonderful way to do this.'

Dorothy offered Darinka a small bowl of freshly made vegetable soup, which was steaming up around her face. The smell of it reminded Darinka of her mother's warm kitchen. Dorothy looked at her intensely. 'You're a wonderful mum, you know. You're more than capable. It just takes a little guidance, a little practice and plenty of patience. And remember… repetition!' Dorothy chuckled. 'If you use my secrets of spontaneous storytelling your whole family will benefit in more ways than you can imagine.' Her eyes danced. She was so vibrant and alive with delight it was infectious.

Darinka ran her fingers through her long brown hair, scratching at her scalp, her head exploding with all this new information. She had been longing for someone to help Adam and her become better parents and promised herself she would come back to hear the other secrets. 'I assume that the first secret is about imagination?'

'Yes, absolutely, spot on,' answered Dorothy. 'Developing and stretching our imaginations.'

The children came back from their hunt, proudly presenting their treasures to Dotty: a little brown acorn in its cup, a dandelion and a large dock leaf.

'Oh, marvellous,' she said. 'Take these treasures home with you and share an ABC story with your dada, using these treasures to help you. But first let's eat and drink. Building dens and telling stories is thirsty work.'

Everyone tucked in. Dorothy poured mint tea for the children too, adding cold water. As they had never tried it before, they were reticent.

"What's this? I don't like it,' said Marija immediately.

'You haven't even tried it, silly,' Tommy responded, looking doubtful himself.

'I like it, it's yum,' Luka beamed.

Later, Dorothy gathered up the picnic remains to take inside. She glanced back at Darinka, who smiled, having been reminded of her own childhood in Slovenia. It was dawning on her how much she had lost sight of her own roots in her attempt to be accepted into Adam's community.

The children were snuggled together. Tommy was playing a finger game in the grass, muttering under his breath. Marija was lying down on her tummy, bent legs waving back and forth, inventing a story with the treasures they'd found. Luka was still eating, jam all over his face.

Darinka was contemplating how she was always trying to fill their time with clubs and activities, feeling like a bad mother if she didn't. She had spoken to other mothers about the pressures they faced and realised that all the expectations stopped their children from having uninterrupted time to explore their creativity. She was surprised how healing it was to be idle together.

The heat had gone out of the sun and the air was cooling rapidly. Darinka realised she needed to get the children home before they became over-tired. This had happened many times, with dire consequences. She didn't want to spoil what had been a near perfect afternoon.

She wanted to tell Adam everything, although she was already afraid he wouldn't be interested. She wanted to inspire him to play story games to encourage the kids' imaginations. She wanted him to understand the importance of storytelling to help improve their literacy skills and as a means of developing their self -confidence. Dorothy had also mentioned how stories could help them to overcome obstacles at school and throughout their lives.

No one wanted to leave, but it was a long walk home. The children gave Dotty a huge, combined hug and she held them in her embrace until they were ready to let go. 'I'm going back to look at your den again in a moment. What a great job you did.'

Tommy was so thrilled he hugged her again.

'Thank you,' said Darinka softy, touching the edge of Dorothy's shawl. 'I feel really nourished'.

Dorothy nodded. 'You're so welcome,' she said. 'It's been a great pleasure for me to spend time with you all.' She turned to Tommy, 'Now, jump on your magic carpet and share an ABC story between you as you travel home'.

'I want to go on the magic carpet!' said Luka.

'There is no magic carpet!' said Marija crossly as Dorothy laid out an imaginary carpet for them to jump on to.

'Here it is, dummy,' Tommy said to his sister,

pulling her towards him. Dorothy blew them all a kiss before turning her back and walking towards the old oak.

Darinka was anxious about how late it was but taking Dorothy's cue to play the ABC story meant there was barely a complaint between them all the way home. Luka asked for a piggyback when their hilarious story finished, but by this time they were crossing the canal bridge.

Adam was in the kitchen when he heard the front door open and he rushed to greet them. 'Where've you been?' he asked, running his hand through his hair anxiously before helping Marija and Luka with their coats and boots.

All three children were talking over each other, pushing and shoving, telling their dad about their day, wanting to show him their treasures.

Darinka gave him a tender kiss.

'I thought you'd left,' he said in an agitated whisper, his eyes staring deeply into hers, searching for an answer. He had come home at lunchtime to find them gone and had spent the afternoon in a state of panic. 'I called you several times. Your phone was switched off.'

'No, I'm here,' said Darinka, stroking his arm. 'You're certainly a prat at times.' They both giggled as he nodded. 'But,' she continued, 'I've learnt a lot today that I want to share with you. First let's get them bathed and into bed.'

Adam grinned broadly, relieved, as he willingly took the lead in the bedtime ritual. He listened, almost in disbelief, as the children told him about their friend Gnomie Blue Hat, the den they had built next to the old oak tree, their treasures and Dotty, their new friend. Luka told him in detail about the jam sandwiches. It took much persuasion and bribery for Darinka to convince them to keep their treasure stories until morning.

'There is such a thing as too many stories,' she chuckled, remembering Dorothy's words as she and Adam tiptoed downstairs. 'Stories are like meals, so I don't want to over-stuff them before sleep time by telling them too many stories at once!'

They sat together on the sofa, Darinka's legs tucked underneath her. She wrapped a fluffy red blanket round her as she shared what Dorothy had told her. Adam listened.

'I'm going to make things simpler for the children if I can,' said Darinka, 'and I'm going to try to find ways to be more present in those moments too. Not distracted on the phone or my computer.' She knew it wasn't easy to achieve, but she had seen just how joyful the children had been in the simplest of settings and wanted to provide this space whenever she could. She was so inspired from the day. All her other concerns were pushed away.

As they headed upstairs to bed Adam asked, 'Who is this Dorothy? Describe her to me again.' Adam was puzzled, he had lived in the village all his life and thought he knew everyone, but he didn't recognise her. Darinka was following him up the stairs as he asked, 'I forgot to ask where you met her?'

'Oh she lives in the windmill at the top of Tupp Hill.'

Adam stopped in his tracks.

'What?' asked Darinka.

'Dinks, why are you lying? The windmill's derelict. You know it's been boarded up for years. It's where Si and I used to play as kids. I was there with him only a month or two ago, nothing's changed. It's only got worse.'

They were both silent.

'But I'm not lying, why would I?' Darinka said sharply, her anger rising in her confusion. Adam said nothing.

'Adam, listen to me, I'm not...' her voice trailed off as she heard the bathroom door slam shut.

Story Games from Chapter 1

A Family with Different Adventures Throughout the Year – see page 39
To share in a family or group setting with as few or many listeners as you like

- Make up a story based around a family, in whatever form that might take, including, for example, a family of animals.
- Make up stories about the adventures of this family as they experience the different seasons, festivals and activities throughout a year.

The children will enjoy the repetition and familiarity, whilst the storyteller can enjoy the changing events. For young children, keep it simple so the family always comes home safely from their travels.

The ABC Game – see page 42
For two or more players

- In a group the first player begins a story with one or two sentences, the first word of which begins with the letter A.
- The story passes to the next player who continues the story, the first word of which starts with the letter B.
- Player three continues with a sentence beginning with the letter C, and so on through the alphabet. The player with the letter Z wraps up the story.
- As the story develops, weaving previous characters or events back into the story is satisfying and can also be very funny.
- If a player is stuck they can ask the group for word examples or they can choose to pass the story to the

next player. I recommend not correcting players if they begin with the wrong letter or make a mistake (S for Ceiling for example).

The more you play the more proficient you will all become, but remember this game is for the fun of the story and not the rules!

Did you know?

- It's great to try new things!
- Exploration is tied to the neurotransmitter dopamine, which also plays a role in motivation and learning, amongst other things. Neuroscientific research shows that being open to new experiences links to our creative thinking. According to Scott Barry Kaufman and Carolyn Gregoire in *Wired to Create: Unraveling the Mysteries of the Creative Mind*, 'The drive for exploration, in its many forms, may be the single most important personal factor predicting creative achievement.'

Further reading...

Wired to Create: Unraveling the Mysteries of the Creative Mind, by Carolyn Gregoire and Scott Barry Kaufman.

Storytelling and the Art of the Imagination, by Nancy Mellon.

CHAPTER 2

Is She for Real?
The Second Secret –
Observation and Senses

'Smell is a potent wizard that transports you across thousands of miles and all the years you have lived.'
Helen Keller

They were both silent as they undressed and got into bed. Adam lay down, turning his back to Darinka. She was cross that he thought she had lied to him and that somehow the children were in on it too. How could he believe that of her? The intimacy they had enjoyed earlier was replaced by tension and frustration. Darinka wanted to take him to the windmill now, to prove that she had met Dorothy, to prove it to herself too. Instead, unwilling to reach out to Adam in the darkness, she lay on her side, motionless, eyes open.

When Luka woke he had tried to take Tommy's stone from the little table in their room but his brother had grabbed it back.

'Get off, it's mine, I found it. Get your own,' Tommy shouted.

Luka kicked his brother and they had begun to wrestle with each other, but the thought of playing the ABC story with his dad distracted Tommy enough to run into his parent's room.

When Tommy dived onto their bed, he was full of stories of their adventures with Dotty. He pulled at the duvet. 'Dada, Dada, I want to tell you our story now. Wake up, Dada.'

Darinka kissed Tommy and after lifting the twins up on to the bed, she slipped downstairs to make drinks.

Adam turned onto his back with his hands behind his head. 'Good morning, trouble,' he yawned and smiled at Tommy.

'Dada, I've got my treasure,' Marija said, holding out the acorn to show him. 'Look.'

Adam sat up and the three children squealed in delight. Usually, at the weekends, their mum took them downstairs to play until Adam woke.

There was no wind this morning. Darinka put down the hot lemon water and a warm fruity tea for the children on their bedside tables before opening the curtains and getting back into bed. Adam screwed up his eyes as bright light streamed into the room. Luka copied his dad. The rain had fallen heavily in the night but now the sky was a deep blue. It was just before 7am.

Darinka planned for them all to walk along the canal after breakfast. Then for Adam to take them to his sister's house to play with their cousin Lucy at 11am.

'Look what I've got,' said Luka, thrusting the wilted dock leaf into his dad's face.

Tommy began imitating Dotty's voice, repeating some of the ideas and words she'd used during their story yesterday. 'It was a misty day, the wind made the old tree wobble like a plate of jelly. The huge windmill at the top of the hill was surrounded by dock leaves. These leaves covered a secret passageway...'

Darinka smiled as she watched the children drawing their dad into the story, passing it back and forth. When the story became disjointed, she took over and wove sections back together, like a tapestry. She was happy to forgo their walk to make way for this special time together.

Luka said that Little Blue Hat was having a tea party, which inspired Marija to run to her room to find small pieces of paper on which to write the invitations. Once they were written, she pushed them through Luka's waiting fingers as if posting them in a letter box. She tugged at her dad's fingers to post more. There was a great deal of laughter as Adam wasn't sure what to do.

'Like this,' said Tommy, grabbing his dad's hand and holding it up for Marija.

'Dada,' said Marija, 'your go. What happened next?'

Adam flinched before dropping his hand and clumsily announcing, 'Come on, it's time for breakfast. Let's get your teeth cleaned and clothes on. We've got a busy day. You're going to Aunty Rach's.'

Marija stuck her tongue out at her dad and Tommy tried to continue the story, but almost immediately Adam interrupted abruptly, 'Okay, tell me how it ends?'

Darinka quickly took over, '...and as the mist lifted, the children said goodbye to little Gnomie. They crawled back up the secret passage from his underground den and sat at the foot of the oak tree. The children were all hungry. It was time for something to eat.'

'The END!' shouted Marija, a defiant glint in her eye. The children jumped off the bed, racing to the bathroom to see who could be first.

Darinka was cross with Adam for being so sharp and snappy. She turned to speak to him as the children left the room. Instead, Adam clapped his hands in an effort to lighten the mood. Throwing on his jeans and t-shirt, he yelled, 'Come on, breakfast time! I'll make bacon and eggs. Let's see if you can get dressed without Mama's help. Then you're off to Aunty Rach's.'

During breakfast, Luka accidentally knocked over his cup, spilling it into his sister's plate of half-eaten toast and honey. Luka squeezed his eyes shut, expecting to be shouted at as Marija's face wrinkled up.

Tommy pointed and called out, 'It's a raft, sailing down the canal...'

Adam joined in, 'Quick, it's sinking. Man overboard, man overboard.'

Marija's shoulders relaxed and Luka opened his eyes, giggling as their mum took the plate away and made another piece of toast.

'Let's build a new raft, shall we?' suggested Adam.

Mealtimes in the Dale household were often stormy, with arguments, admonishments and tears. Adam's temper rose quickly as he attempted to discipline them.

'Leave the table this instant. Come back when you can behave better!' he'd scream, pointing to one or other of the children, leading to more tears.

'They need to learn,' he'd say crossly to Darinka when she defended them or tried to calm the situation. 'You're much too soft on them. How will they ever learn manners if we don't tell them?'

This morning had been different and Adam was relaxed.

Whilst Adam was in the kitchen, the phone rang. It was Rachel.

'Hello, lovely,' she said to Darinka. 'I'm sorry, Lucy's not having a good day. She's woken up anxious. It's not going to work for us. Could we make it another day? Maybe Tuesday, after school?'

'Sure, of course,' said Darinka. 'Is there anything I can do? Tuesday isn't good, Tommy has swimming, maybe Friday?'

'Okay, yes. No, we'll manage. Let's speak in the week.'

Darinka put the phone down, sighing heavily. She'd been looking forward to a day with Adam, particularly as she wanted to take him up to the windmill to meet Dorothy.

'Who was it?' Adam called from the kitchen.

Darinka broke the news, worried about the effect it would have on Tommy in particular; he loved playing with his cousin who was in the same year as him at school.

Lucy had been given an early, but inconclusive, autism diagnosis so Rachel and David were waiting for a re-assessment to access the additional help they need-ed to support their daughter. Rachel thought this im-pending meeting was making Lucy more agitated than usual. Darinka only mentioned this to Adam when they were on their own, washing up after breakfast.

Adam changed the subject, not wanting to hear about it. 'I can't believe how chilled the kids were this morning,' he said. 'I thought Marija would kick off when Luka's water flooded her toast, didn't you?' They both laughed.

One of the things Darinka loved most about Adam was his mischievous giggle.

'Okay,' announced Adam to the children when they came back into the sitting room, 'so as you're not going to Aunty Rach's, we've got a job to do. We're go-ing to clear out Squidge Room.'

Adam had built this small room, which adjoined their sitting room, as part of the rear extension a num-ber of years ago. It was piled high with boxes, furniture, baby clothes and forgotten toys. They called it Squidge Room because when Tommy was younger his dad had told him it was so crammed full, he was the only one small enough to squeeze into it.

Tommy had repeated, 'I only one who squidge it,' pointing his finger to himself. His parents had laughed about it many times and the name had stuck.

It had been on their list to clear it out for a long time, to turn it into a playroom and make more space in the sitting room. Darinka was delighted!

'My secret den,' declared Luka, unaware of the magnitude of the task ahead.

All morning they worked together. It was like a military operation. The sitting room was divided into four areas – one for things to be recycled or thrown away, one for the charity shop, one for keeping and the fourth area was allocated for the children to sort through their toys, deciding which ones to keep.

Adam carried some of the larger items to his van, giving them an immediate sense of achievement. Darinka worked slowly, sorting through baby things, memories flooding back as she laboured over which pile to put each item. They had decided not to have another baby but it was hard for her to let go of some things, especially a couple of Tommy's first sleepsuits which she had reused for the twins.

Adam said irritably, 'You're taking so long! Just take them all to the charity shop, Dinks. Someone will be able to use them instead of them being boxed up here, gathering dust.'

She knew he was right but it didn't make it easier.

By lunchtime mounds of stuff were strewn across the sitting room, but the Squidge Room was accessible. They stopped to have a drink. Marija was holding an abacus, trying to work out how to use it.

'Mine,' yelled Luka, running across the room, snatching it out of his sister's hand.

'No, it's not, it's mine,' said Tommy. 'Give it to me.'

'Don't snatch, either of you!' snapped Darinka. 'It's lunchtime. Luka come with me to chop some carrots.' As she took Luka's hand, she suggested to Adam that after lunch they could get some fresh air before carrying on. To her surprise Adam told her that he was taking the rubbish to the dump.

'Not before lunch, sweetie,' she answered quietly, so Luka didn't hear. 'Go later when we've done more clearing.'

'Need to get there before it closes,' Adam said, not caring whether the children heard or not.

'But it doesn't close till 4pm,' Darinka reasoned, still whispering.

'No,' Adam exploded, getting up to put his sweat-shirt and boots on. 'I'm going now.'

Tommy jumped up too, dropping the abacus. 'I'm coming with you, Dada.'

'No, you're not,' responded Adam without a beat. 'It's lunchtime. Anyway, I need to swing by the site to pick up my stuff to get those shelves up.'

'I want to help you, Dada,' Tommy pleaded. He loved going with his dad in the van and hearing stories about work.

'I said, NO! And I mean, NO!' Adam snapped back.

Darinka's temper rose too. 'What's wrong with you? Why do you have to shout so much? Just go!'

Tommy ran to his mother who wrapped her arms around him. Her heart was pounding and her jaw was clenched. She let out a huge sigh to try to release it. She couldn't understand why Adam was always running away.

Adam slammed the door behind him. 'Bloody hell!' he shouted. Almost immediately he was furious with himself. Why was it that he could go for weeks without a raised word and then seemingly out of nowhere, the slightest thing made him explode? He drove straight to the dump, but it was the thought of the windmill, its sails turning, which had been nagging at the back of his mind, building like a pressure cooker inside him. He needed to know.

The windmill couldn't possibly be open he reasoned, but he had to see for himself and find out who this Dorothy woman was...

Parking his van close to the snicket, he headed over the bridge towards the fields. The heavy clay mud, caused by the overnight rain, stuck firmly to his boots making it hard to walk at any pace. As he approached the hill, the wind blew the drizzle into his face causing him to bow his head, but for a split second he thought he had seen the sails turning. He pushed against the wind but as he neared the building he clearly saw the graffitied, boarded door, the bricked-up windows and the once shiny black paint splitting and peeling from the walls.

He felt his anger rise in his chest, thumping in his heart and pounding in his head. Why would Darinka lie to him and how could she get the kids to make up such an elaborate story? He couldn't make any sense of it. Was she punishing him, getting back at him for their arguments?

In his confusion he carried on, walking beyond the mill, striding ever upwards. It was as if a tight band was contracting around his chest, causing him to catch his breath and gasp, but he pushed on. He was heading for Echo Hollow, a mighty sunken dip where he had hidden from the world as a child when his mum went away.

His mum had struggled to bring up the two children alone and regularly left him and Rachel with their gran when she went on tour, as a dancer in the chorus of a travelling theatre company. He would also hide in the hollow to avoid his mum's fury when he flunked at school or got into some trouble or other.

These memories flashed through his head as he sat on the edge of the crater, breathing deeply, trying to stop the pain in his chest. This was his safe place and he had been so pleased to show it to Darinka on one of her early visits.

'It's a *Vrtača*,' she had yelled out in pleasure, throwing her arms round his neck and kissing him all over his face. He had giggled with joy as she had explained that it was like one of the Karst sinkholes at home.

Meeting Darinka had made his life brighter. She had a way of getting him out of the emotional sinkholes he repeatedly fell into.

They had agreed it was their own secret *Vrtača*, a place just for them.

As Adam sat there, the drizzle soaking through his coat, he realised they hadn't been here since before the twins were born. He was conflicted and confused. He had to find a way to control his temper. It was pushing Darinka away. As he thought about her leaving, the band across his chest constricted again and he took several sharp intakes of breath.

He slipped over the edge of the crater, sliding down the grass on his back, trying to stretch out and relax and avoid this kind of thinking. Down at the bottom of the hollow was an area protected from the rain by a protruding boulder. The wind was thrashing and whistling, scattering the heavy grey and fluffy white clouds across the sky.

He sat up with a jump, his heart thumping fast from the shock. A woman with a gentle smiling face and a mass of reddy-grey hair, piled up in a knot at the back of her head, sat on the slope next to him. Although he'd never seen her before he knew instantly that it was Dorothy from Darinka's description.

'Hello Adam,' she said, before he had caught his breath.

'Who the hell are you? How did you get here?' he asked rudely.

'I'm Dorothy. I met your lovely family yesterday,' she said, ignoring his question. 'You must be so proud of them.' She was disarming, rendering him speechless. 'I wonder what's on your mind? The clouds come and go don't they, like our thoughts. Are yours filled with thunder clouds or are they more like the fluffy, bright ones?'

Adam was determined not to speak. Why should he when she had caused such trouble between Darinka and him. He was seething.

But in the stillness of the hollow as they sat side by side, his anger slowly gave way to relief that Darinka had not lied to him about her. She was at least real, even if the Windmill was boarded up.

He glanced over at her, sitting on a large pink and orange woollen shawl. She was smiling and he remembered Darinka describing her tranquillity. His thoughts bounced between wanting to tell her to get lost and storming off himself. He remained tight-lipped, listening to the ticking of his watch, unable to get her question out of his head. He went over and over in his thoughts what he might say to her if she spoke again but, like his nan, she sat quietly next to him, unperturbed by his struggles. Eventually, as if against his will, he found himself speaking. He spat out the words, angrily, wanting to shock her. 'I'm a terrible father and a useless partner, so I'm definitely one of your storm clouds.'

'May I stay for a while?' Dorothy asked quietly, waiting for his reply.

Adam cracked his knuckles one by one and picked at his finger. He thought about how differently the kids had behaved that morning, maybe as a result of the stories Dorothy had shared yesterday. He had upset Darinka again today and even he could see that, if he did not get some help, it was only a matter of time before she left him. On top of all this he could not help being a little curious about this odd woman. He nodded his head, almost imperceptibly.

Dorothy's smile broadened as she spoke. 'Maybe we can play a game to help clear those thoughts, so you can see what lies beyond them?'

Adam's instinct was to bolt but somehow, caught under her spell, she reminded him of his nan who had always been there for him despite him pushing her away.

Dorothy asked him to describe what he saw in the sky.

Silently he thought how stupid this was, like being back at school. Again, he wanted to leave, but part of Tommy's story popped into his head, so he spoke, slowly and moodily, whilst looking up at the sky.

'The thick clouds are beginning to break up, making way for some wispy peaks and some deep heavy masses.'

Dorothy encouraged him with her own commentary, 'Can you see that dragon charging towards that cloud? Oh, and there's a turtle, or is it... is it a Ferrari?'

This made him laugh. 'Can't be a Ferrari, it hasn't got a low enough chassis!' Adam grinned as Dorothy's eyes danced.

'Ah yes, I see that now, but the dragon's turned into a whale and is now eating peas. Can you see that?' she asked, as if laying down a challenge.

Adam, rising to the challenge, stared up at the sky intently.

Dorothy continued, 'North Wind has those birds scattering, like torpedoes, across the skies.'

Adam was furiously searching the sky. 'Ah... ah! There's a... over there, on a, a... a chariot. Can you see— there,' chuckled Adam, pointing upwards and across.

Their banter continued until his eyes locked gaze with hers for a just a moment. A light wind swept across his face. He sighed heavily as his brow unfurrowed.

As the blue sky began to reveal itself, Adam could smell the damp air and hear the thunder of a plane.

'I know it can seem childish, but I'm always amazed how stories can help us to relax and enjoy being carefree again,' Dorothy explained quietly. 'They're powerful when they emerge from what we see, hear, touch or smell around us.'

He thought again how calm it had been at breakfast and wondered if this was a result of the story they'd shared in bed. He pondered for a moment before answering. 'I didn't know I could do that. I was rubbish at making up stories when I was a kid. They made us write everything down. I wasn't interested in books and I still don't like reading... I just wanted to be outside.'

'Ah, you can create incredible stories for your children using this love of nature and your wonderful climbing, exploring, building skills.'

Adam's head dropped, he found it hard to hear this. His throat tightened. 'I just don't know how to be a dad.'

He told her that he had never met his own father and when he had asked his mum about his father, she had made a thoughtless comment after a couple of large whiskeys. 'I've no flippin' idea darlin,' she'd said. 'It could be any one of a dozen to be honest – none of them any good.' These words had haunted Adam.

'It wasn't great to hear this from her, to be honest.' Adam squeezed his left hand into a fist, opening and closing it as he continued. 'But I thought I'd let go of that a long time ago. I wasn't close to Mum but in those last few years before we lost her, I realised that she was okay to be fair. She did her best.'

Rachel had never forgiven her mum and they hadn't spoken since Rachel had left home at 17. Although their mum had left everything, including her house, to Adam he had taken out a mortgage in order that his sister received her share.

'When I met Darinka, I made a vow that my kids would have a proper father.' His voice trailed off as if he was speaking to himself. 'I'm not sure I'm up to it, to be honest. Sometimes I wish we hadn't had kids. Things were much better between Dinks and me before

Tommy arrived. I'm on the outside – it's Darinka and them against me.'

Adam hadn't voiced this before, his face flushed red momentarily, but he continued. 'The twins made it much worse. I could just about cope with one – Tommy's not as demanding. But hell, they cry and yell all the time. And Luka's started biting and kicking. It drives me mad.'

A large buzzard circled overhead, the sun broke through the clouds and the birds chatted and sang.

Dorothy somehow made him feel safe enough to speak his innermost fears. Her kindness was palpable. With every guilty thought he shared he could feel the band loosening from around his chest.

Finally, he said, 'It's just easier to stay away, but I know that doesn't help. I hate the arguments – it reminds me of how crazy my mum was. Different men came and went, she's shouted and screamed at them and at Rach and me too. She threw a plate at me once.' Adam rubbed at a small, raised, white scar just below his lip. He stopped speaking but, when Dorothy still said nothing, he continued, uncomfortable with the silence. 'I'm all alone. I miss how it was with Dinks back then.' Adam clenched his fists and his jaw, feeling exposed and wanting to run, but he didn't move. He could hear his heart beating in his chest.

Eventually Dorothy spoke, purposefully, 'Well, it's true a father's task isn't an easy one and we certainly don't like to hear about men struggling, do we? It can be lonely as you hold the space, like an umbrella, over the top of mother and baby. It won't always be like this, but right now I wonder if you could bear the pain of it for a little longer as Darinka focuses on the children? Sometimes we have to look closely underneath or beyond the screams and tears to discover what the child's real need is – whether they're hungry, tired, in need of undivided attention or perhaps a firm boundary. Darinka needs you to travel side by side with her, but the two of you have different, complementary, tasks right now. I think you're up to it.' Dorothy winked at Adam and gave him a little, cheeky nudge, which made him relax.

This image of him being the umbrella protecting his partner and children was powerful. It gave him a sense of purpose and he thought to himself that if he really did have an important role to play, he wanted to step up to the task. 'How can I tell stories to the kids? I don't even know where to begin?' he suddenly asked.

'There are many ways,' Dorothy began. 'But I suggest you use what comes easily to you. You love being outside, in nature. So, by consciously observing your surroundings, activating your five senses, you'll open the door to your stories. I have no doubt that you can create some wonderful, dynamic tales, which the children will love.'

Adam wasn't convinced but he was ready to try. Darinka had mentioned Dorothy's suggestion to make up a story about a family and he wondered if he could do this. He'd enjoyed being with the children in bed, hearing their laughter as they made up a story together.

'I saw yesterday that Tommy also has a love of the outdoors, doesn't he? He's longing for you to share your world with him, Adam.' Dorothy didn't hold her punches.

Adam took a sharp intake of breath and recoiled, a tear shot up into his eye as he pulled at the wet grass with his hand, remembering Tommy's plea this morning and many other mornings.

'I'm coming with you, Dada, let me come.'

Dorothy, sensing his pain, distracted him by asking him to describe the hollow in which they sat without considering it to be a story.

Adam could not speak, as his stomach turned. When she prompted him again, he said, 'It started as a damp, drizzly day, but this canny wind pushed the heavy clouds across the sky, opening them up like a thick metal door, the blue sky behind it. That buzzard's looking for a mouse.' It was easier than he imagined and certainly diverted his thoughts. Adam held his arm up above his head, moving it in slow circles, imitating the bird, as he continued. 'He can see far into the distance and can swoop down to grab his prey in his clutches and take it home to feed his babies.' Adam smiled, letting his arm drop rapidly, swooping down and making a talon from his fingers. He was enjoying the play of it all, his voice becoming ominous. 'For a moment he wondered if I was good bait, but this is my Vrtača, my safe place, there's no way he can get me here.'

'Well, there you are, at the beginning of your story,' laughed Dorothy.

Adam could have gone on, although it didn't seem much of a story. Dorothy assured him that if he had begun that story and couldn't think of how to continue, the children would have jumped in with plenty of suggestions.

Adam snorted. 'That's true. Between them, they're

never lost for words! But wouldn't that be a bit gory for Marija and Luka?'

'What you'd be sharing is your love of nature. Not scary for scary's sake. Keep it light and playful and make sure that you bring them to a safe and happy conclusion at the end of your story. This way they'll take all the goodness from it.

'Try to remember that little children don't need you to tell the story in a way that's dramatic, with big voices or threatening sounds. If they were here and could see the buzzard as you told your story, then all the better. Then at home you can make up more stories about the buzzard. Buzzard could become their friend. You'll be amazed at how this activates their imaginations and how quickly they'll use the language you've shared with them. And remember, pet, use not only what you see but also what you smell, touch, taste and hear.'

Like the sky, Adam was beginning to brighten.

Dorothy continued, 'Many of us suffer from sensory overload in our modern life, particularly children. Take a shopping centre as an example.'

'Urgh, I hate taking them shopping... I hate shopping!' Adam interjected. Dorothy laughed and nodded, sweeping a strand of hair back into place.

'I'm not surprised, pet. The cacophony of noise, but also the excessive choices on offer, the visual overload, the smells and the intensity of so many people in one place. While we, as adults, tune out to it all, small children feel everything acutely. They can be overwhelmed.'

Adam could hear irritation in Dorothy's voice that he hadn't noticed before.

She paused for a moment to compose herself, and as she did so she knocked her green lace-up boots together. 'Well, this manifests in what we call a tantrum. This is them attempting to release the overload through their screams. Look, pet, it's affecting me just talking about it!'

They both laughed.

Adam recognised what she was describing – he could smell the cleaning fluids used in their local shopping centre, mingled with the bready smell from the pie shop and see the garish fluorescent lighting, his kids having kicked off many times in the past. If he had to take them with him he was usually irritated, but when they screamed he got seriously angry with them. As he listened to Dorothy, he realised he'd made an awful event much worse.

'So, what can I do in a situation like this? We have to take them sometimes, there's no choice,' he said.

Dorothy nodded, considering the question. 'For young children we can create big, interesting, extraordinary worlds in our stories but then, by finishing the story in a gentle, quiet way, bringing them back home, they will feel safe. When they hear stories of people who have adventures and overcome challenges it can give them the confidence to face their own day-to-day tasks, knowing that at home they are protected and loved.'

Adam frowned as he tried to put what she was saying into his own context. He couldn't think how he could ever make up a story the kids would like.

'So, let's see.' Dorothy picked up on his thoughts. 'On your way to the supermarket you could tell them a story, for example about Aladdin's Cave and all the jewels that are in the cave. Aladdin has asked you to find certain jewels and to leave all the rest where they are for other adventurers. If you ask Tommy to hold the list of jewels – which of course is your shopping list – he can then tell you when they've discovered one of the treasures.'

Aladdin was one of Adam's favourite stories as a child. Dorothy made it all seem so easy.

'Of course, this story could change each time you go. Or you could add to the same one over time.'

'Luka will want the same one over and over,' Adam interrupted.

'Yes, pet, the repetition will make him feel safe. Repetition is so important for young children as it forms the basis of their memory. For example, when you remind him to brush his teeth, morning and evening, he absorbs that into who he is and then as he gets older, he will continue to brush his teeth. When we share stories, we can gently help them to learn how to care for themselves, for their environment and for others. No nagging, no moralising. And remember, pet, when you add descriptions of the senses, smells, tastes, sounds, you'll make up better stories.'

Dorothy went on to explain that using the senses in a conscious way would help calm the children after a meltdown, fright or argument.

When Adam asked for examples, Dorothy mentioned smelling an orange, a flower or fresh washing, or by observing something for a minute or so, such as a spider spinning its web, a bird, or an ant. By touching the grass with their feet or hands, tasting the juice of a cherry, hugging a tree, holding a soft blanket...

'If you get them to touch, observe or smell two or three things, one after the other, it'll bring them back into themselves,' Dorothy chuckled. 'You don't even need nice smells!'

Adam giggled.

'Let's play a game with this idea,' Dorothy suggested. 'That way you'll remember it when you most need it!'

'How?' asked Adam.

'Okay, let's use observation. Each person chooses something to observe, like the spider I mentioned earlier.'

Adam remarked that he couldn't see Marija staying still for even a moment.

'Yes, it's certainly a test of her stamina. If you let her know that it isn't an easy task, she may well enjoy rising to that challenge.'

Adam smiled. His little firecracker daughter definitely liked a challenge.

'Remember, you're not asking her to sit still or be quiet. You're asking her to watch something closely. If you try this for yourself, you'll see it's harder than you think to watch something exclusively for any prolonged period of time. The point of the game isn't to see who can stare for the longest but who can use their observation skills to create a story, use it as a springboard into a tale – just like you did with the clouds.'

Adam decided he'd be useless at the game. He hated to sit still, but he reckoned Luka, who really enjoyed sitting and staring, would love the game.

'It really doesn't much matter how long they stay focused,' continued Dorothy, 'but you'll probably find that, if you and they enjoy the game, you'll all be still for longer periods each time you play.

'This game has so many benefits beyond strength-ening your storytelling skills. A minute each day spent observing will create rich and textured stories, but you'll also find yourselves calmer and more content as a happy side effect!' Dorothy had a way of answer-ing questions that Adam hadn't even asked. 'Sensory overload can leave us feeling either over-stimulated or empty. When we begin to really observe with our sens-es it brings us back to the present moment.'

Dorothy told him that when her grandchildren were little, they'd initiated the observing game for themselves in the park.

'To make up a story, start with something you love or feel passionately about,' Dorothy suggested gently.

It reminded Adam of a time when he had put Tommy on his shoulders and taken him outside to watch the stars. He had wanted to share it with his son, but Tommy, who would have been around four years old, wasn't interested.

'How many times did you take him to look?' asked Dorothy.

'Once!' Adam laughed at himself. 'Darinka teas-es me when I say, "I've told the children to clean their teeth once, why do I have to keep telling them?"'

Dorothy laughed too. 'So maybe you could try star-gazing again?'

Adam nodded. 'Actually, after swimming last week Tommy pointed to the crescent moon and said he could see the other side of it. I was on the phone so I didn't take much notice.'

There was so much wisdom in her words but he wasn't convinced that it would work with his kids, even if he could remember everything. He shuddered with cold, shuffling to make himself more comfortable, his wet jeans stuck to his legs.

'So, have you just shared your second secret with me?' Adam asked flippantly.

'Yes, pet, I have,' she said. 'The power of observation and the use of your five senses.'

Dorothy stood up, dusting down her deep-blue velvet skirt and wrapping her tatty shawl around her once more.

Adam stretched and yawned. He rubbed each foot, twisting them round to get the blood flowing again. As he did, he continued, 'Oh, I meant to tell you, the kids made up a story this morning with the...' but as he looked up, Dorothy had gone.

He jumped up, one foot throbbing with pins and needles, and scrambled as quickly as he could up the hollow to see where she had gone. At the top of *Vrtača* he looked round but couldn't see her anywhere.

As he walked home the light was fading fast. He was annoyed that, having accepted her so readily, she had disappeared without a word. But he knew that if Darinka asked if he liked the strange woman he would have to answer yes.

He paused outside their front door, knocking clumps of clay off his boots and bending down to unlace them. Darinka and the children were at the table, finishing tea. The sitting room was much tidier than when he had left.

Marija and Luka, already in their pyjamas, ran towards him, calling and pulling at his sleeve.

Darinka folded her arms and stared at him over the rim of her glasses as he crossed the room. Tommy copied his mum, folding his arms too. Adam touched her arm gently as he walked past her and into the utility room with his muddy boots.

'Come see our den, Dada,' demanded Marija.

The green carpet in Squidge Room was visible, although there were still lots of toys, furniture and dust. Adam knelt down, opening his arms to embrace the twins, grateful for their instant love. 'Wow, this is a great room, isn't it?'

'Yes, Dada, and look the spiders have more room now!' Marija pointed to a thick, tangled mass of cobwebs in the corner. 'Mama says that's your job since you weren't here to help.'

Adam laughed as he squeezed Marija close to him. 'Well, Mama is right isn't she?' He spoke loud enough for Darinka to hear.

He came back into the sitting room. 'Fancy a cuppa, Dinks?'

Darinka nodded, tight lipped.

'It's not Squidge Room anymore, Dada. We can all get into it now,' said Marija, in a matter-of-fact way.

Her dad smiled, lifting her into his arms and kissing her forehead.

'We're having popcorn, Dada,' said Luka, pulling his jeans.

'Oh, that's good,' said Adam. 'Let's play the popcorn game, shall we?'

Darinka's mouth opened in disbelief and she stared at him as he headed into the kitchen.

'Come on Dinks, let's play that game with the

children, with popcorn,' he repeated as he placed a steaming mug of tea in front of her.

Darinka had tried to teach him one of her favourite childhood games when they first met, but he had dismissed it as childish. The children asked what it was, but before she had a chance to speak Adam sat down, picking up a piece of popcorn from the large wooden bowl in the centre of the table.

'It's a game your mama used to play when she was your age.' Adam leant over to touch Darinka's hand, cupped around her mug. 'They'll love it, won't they Dinks?' He looked deeply into her eyes and mouthed, 'Sorry.'

Darinka softened, reaching out to pick up a piece of corn. 'Tommy, hold a piece up to the light. What shape is it? Mine is a bumblebee.' Darinka demonstrated, making a buzzing noise as she moved her popcorn round like a bee.

'It's a piece of popcorn,' said Luka.

Tommy snorted. 'Not in the game it's not, silly. It's – it's – it's –' He stared at the piece he had in his hand, wanting to find something to make his dad laugh. 'It's a flying marshmallow.'

Both his parents burst into laughter.

Marija took a piece. 'It's a fly,' she said.

'It's a moon crater,' said Adam, before dropping it into his mouth. 'Now it's going into the black hole!'

The children giggled in delight.

Darinka chuckled too, delighted that the children seemed to like the game as much as she had as a child. 'It's a bead from a necklace.'

They took turns, each of them calling out a new

suggestion before eating it, until the bowl was empty. Afterwards the children ran off to Squidge Room, leaving Adam and Darinka sitting opposite each other at the table.

'I'm sorry, Dinks.' He paused before continuing. 'I never got it before, but it's just like cloud watching, isn't it?'

Adam amazed her; just when she thought it was all over, he would somehow find a way to open her up again. 'You've met her haven't you?'

Adam grinned. 'But not at the windmill...' Before she had chance to ask, he called out, 'I've got another game for you, come on.'

Tommy raced back to the table.

'Let's clear these first,' Adam said, gathering the plates and heading for the kitchen, followed by Tommy who had picked up the salt and pepper grinders. 'Twinnies, sit there and wait. You too Dinks, whilst Tommy helps me clear away,' he instructed. 'Play I -spy or something.'

When he returned, he was carrying a large white plate filled with small cubes of apple, tiny slithers of cucumber and round slices of carrot. Tommy brought through the plate of grapes and lemon slices.

'It's the Taste Test Game. Go and find something to cover your eyes – you need blindfolds,' he announced.

Tommy ran back to the kitchen to grab a tea towel. Darinka went off to find something suitable for the twins.

As he gave each of them a tiny piece of food to taste, Adam asked them in turn to tell him what it was before describing it. The game was serious, hilarious, thoughtful and silly in turn.

Adam said to Darinka later, when the children were fast asleep, 'It's such a simple thing to do together isn't it, but they loved it, didn't they? They went to bed so... so... satisfied. I didn't know if they'd think it was too silly.' There was genuine surprise in his voice.

'They loved doing something with you,' replied Darinka quietly. 'I loved doing something with you. All of us together.'

He leant over and kissed her. 'Sorry Dinks, I'm a prat sometimes.'

'Sometimes?' Darinka smiled broadly, poking him in the ribs. 'Tell me what she said?' Darinka had been dying to hear more.

Adam talked and talked, pouring out the whole encounter, trying not to forget anything. He was more engaged and animated than Darinka had seen him in an age.

'I didn't want to talk to her, Dinks, I wanted to tell her to sod off, but she reminded me of my nan, and she was so, so, not like anyone at the same time. Do you know what I mean?'

Darinka nodded, so relieved he had met her.

'But, is she for real? I mean, who is she, actually? Why haven't I heard of her before?'

Darinka twisted a strand of her hair around her fingers as she thought back to her meeting and the windmill, which Adam confirmed was boarded up when he walked past it. 'Well, none of it makes any sense.' Darinka held out her hand and Adam readily took it into his own. 'It doesn't make sense, but part of me thinks that it doesn't matter who she is. I mean she's already made a difference. Does it matter, if she can help us?'

'Yes... Well, no... no, maybe it doesn't,' Adam agreed. 'Whoever she is, I'm going to try making up a story about a family who have different adventures together through the year. I like the idea of Aladdin's cave. What do you reckon?'

'I reckon it's a great idea, you'll smash it!' Darinka leant over and kissed him.

Her encouragement loosened the knot in the pit of his stomach. Until this moment, he hadn't been aware it was there. He shared Dorothy's metaphor of the umbrella with Darinka, which allowed him to admit his feelings of inadequacy as a father, his fears of failure and letting her down.

'Sometimes I feel like you guys don't need me, that it's the four of you against me. But Dinks, I know it's me that's pushing you away. I'm scared you'll leave.'

Darinka moved closer to him on the sofa, ran her fingers through his hair, stroked his face and kissed his eyelids softly. '*Dragi moj*, I'm staying. I'm here for the long haul.'

STORY GAMES FROM CHAPTER 2

The Cloud Game – see page 67
Alone or with others – in pairs or small groups

- Find a comfortable spot outside to lie down on your back, looking up to the sky – alternatively you could look out of a window.
- Observe the clouds moving across the sky, morphing from one shape to another. Take it in turns to point out the faces, animals, objects, places that you can see. Then make connections between the different images that each player sees, creating a scene.
- Finally choose an image to springboard into a story and use subsequent shapes to inform the story as you create it.
- You can take it in turns to make up a story or share it between you, similar to the ABC story from Chapter One.

The Observation Game – see page 75
Alone or with others – ideal for sharing in groups of two or three

- Choose something to observe, such as an ant, bird, cobweb, flower, your fingers, a chair.
- Study it closely and in silence, engaging other relevant senses such as your hearing, smell or touch as well as your sight.
- Set yourself a short time, perhaps one minute, to remain focused.
- When you have finished your observation, share what you studied with another player, experimenting with the description out loud.
- Swap over to hear your partner's account.

- Now use your observation as the opening to a tale or weave it into a story to enliven the tale.

The more you observe the more words, images and descriptions you will collect to enrich your future stories.

This game has benefits beyond strengthening your storytelling skills including improving concentration and focus, feeling calmer, more content and ready to face your day.

The Popcorn Game – see page 79

For two or more players
- All that is required are players and a bowl of popcorn!
- Each player takes it in turns to hold a piece of popcorn.
- Once they've observed it, using their imagination to decide what it represents, they share this knowledge with the group. For example: a spaceship, an earring, a tennis ball, a piece of ear wax!
- The player then eats the popcorn to signify the next player's turn.
- Continue until you're all full, or the bowl of popcorn is empty.

You could add an additional rule, to help players listen better. The player can only decide 'what it is' when it's their turn, so that anything they think of in advance is not allowed.

The Taste Test Game – see page 80

For two or more players
Please be very cautious of food allergies with this game.
- Assemble a plate filled with small cubes or slices of food with varying tastes and textures, taking into

consideration the five basic tastes of sweet, sour, salty, bitter, and umami.
- Blindfold each of the players before offering each of them a tiny piece of food to smell and taste.
- In turn ask them to tell you what it was, and then to describe the smell and taste of each food.

As with the Observation Game above, use these descriptions to enrich future stories.

Did you know?
- Taste and smell are innately intertwined because our sense of taste is actually 90 percent smell.
- Aphantasia is a condition which prevents a person from being able to picture objects in the mind's eye.
- In 2005, a patient advised Dr Adam Zeman, a cognitive neurologist, that following his surgery, he no longer had the ability to form mental images. Zeman found more people with this condition and named the condition Aphantasia, from the Greek word *phantasia*, which means imagination.

Further reading...
The Man who Tasted Words: Inside the Strange and Startling World of Our Senses, by Dr Guy Leschziner.

CHAPTER 3

There was Silence
The Third Secret – Memory

'Memory is the diary that we all carry about with us.'
Oscar Wilde

As autumn turned to winter Adam was working on the big house on the green, Rowan Court. The whole house had been gutted and stripped and with budgets tightening, there were only three of them left to finish the restoration – including Si, who was doing all the plumbing. They had both expected the job to be finished by the end of summer.

It was the start of another week. Adam was sitting in the corner of the temporary portacabin, eating his elevenses of a cheese and pickle sandwich and home-made pork pie from Acorn Farm Shop.

He was thinking about the kids and how, since he had started to play games with them, they were scream-ing and fighting less. Dorothy had made him aware of how much influence he had on the mood of his family.

'The only thing you can change in a child under seven is their environment,' she had told him. This concept had played around in his mind over and again. He was wrestling with it, disagreeing with it, testing it.

Although he didn't spend much time with them, particularly during the week, Luka was constantly looking for treasure since Adam had played the Aladdin's Cave game in the supermarket, and it only took a small prompt from Tommy at bedtime for them to make up a story together. He was chuffed with himself for telling a tale about the brightest star cluster, the *Pleiades*. Although Tommy had helped quite a lot! He didn't find it easy, but he was getting better at it all the time.

Dorothy had also said, 'Imagination is like a muscle – the more you use it, the stronger it becomes.'

This had stimulated his curiosity. He smiled at the memory of Luka pointing to a piece of thread on the carpet one morning as he helped his son to get dressed. Luka called out gleefully, 'Look, Dada. It's Incy Wincy 'pider.'

Before meeting Dorothy, Adam would have told Luka it was a piece of fluff but instead he'd responded, 'Oh yes, Incy Wincy Spider lives in *Babica's* big, old silver teapot. He's climbed up and out of the spout to search for a fly to take back to his family to eat for their breakfast.'

Luka was delighted. 'Tell me about 'pider, Dada.'

It was over two months since he'd met Dorothy, yet the effect of her secrets on his family was evident. Dorothy had been so encouraging and kind to him and the advice she had given him about using his experiences of being outdoors in all weathers had made it much easier for him not only to make up tales with the kids but to enjoy being with them. He wanted to learn more.

Although the pressure of work never stopped, he made time to walk with the children along the canal after school when he could, or play frisbee in the fields at the weekends. Darinka had commented that he wasn't staying at work so late or going to the pub as often and they were fighting less.

Adam had set up a challenge for Tommy to get him to cycle up and down the hills between the rows of houses.

'Just to the next lamppost mate, you can do it,' he had encouraged Tommy, as the little boy, red-faced and determined, struggled to get from one post to the next, desperate to please his dad. When he reached the top he was triumphant.

This extra time Adam spent with the kids meant that Darinka, fluent in German, could offer a few private tutoring lessons for GCSE German students in the area and she relished the opportunity.

'I can't believe how inventive Tommy is,' Darinka had said to Adam last weekend as they walked home from the woods. 'Before, when I told him a story on our way to school he would keep interrupting, telling me I was wrong. It was tiring. But when I started to add in the sound of a car or the smell of a bonfire – like Dorothy suggested to you – he listened intently. It completely changed the story for him.' Darinka continued, 'Dorothy's like a child whisperer. I wonder when we'll see her again?'

'Or where!' Adam had added as they both laughed.

He thought about how brilliant Darinka was at what Tommy called, *Dotty Stories*, and about how they were both incorporating them into their daily life.

As Adam ate the last of his pie, thinking about his family, a text brought him out of this state of reverie. He wiped his hands on his jeans, licked his lips and picked up his phone.

Can you confirm when you're fitting the barn doors? Concerned about the frosts. Will you start on Monday as planned? Becs

There were so many texts he hadn't responded to:

Can I have that quote for felling the tree you looked at last week? When are you free to do it? J

Hi Adam, the plaster's dry now, so wonder when you can finish the job?

Give me a call, pal. Need a hand on this next one.

Adam put his phone in his pocket and headed back to the house to fit the final section of architrave in the kitchen. He passed Si on his way upstairs, carrying the new taps.

'Come for a pint with me at the Crown after?' Si asked.

'Okay.' Adam frowned, puzzled. 'Anything wrong?'

Si continued up the stairs without replying.

'See you there then, mate?' Adam called up the stairs.

Si, without looking round, lifted his thumb by way of confirmation.

Adam was worried, it was really unlike Si to suggest the pub midweek. Shubu, Si's wife, had been diagnosed with stage one breast cancer at the beginning of the year. Darinka had told him that Shubu had been rushed into hospital over the weekend with a severe chest infection.

'I'm waiting to hear,' she'd told Adam on Sunday evening when he asked whether she had been discharged. 'I tried her earlier but her phone's switched off.'

Shubu was a teacher at New Park Primary, the children's school. She and Darinka had joined a yoga class in the village hall when Si first introduced them. The women had got on well straightaway, and after one particularly silly giggling episode at the back of class cemented their friendship, they had been best friends ever since.

Adam had forgotten to ask Si when he arrived at work that morning, so was itching to finish so he could find out the news. He texted Darinka to let her know he would be home late. He didn't expect her to text back because she was tutoring all afternoon and then taking the kids to a combined gym n' swim class in their local pool, with Rachel and Lucy.

Adam and Si sat opposite each other, in the garden at their local. It was dark and the air was sharp with cold. Neither of them had spoken or moved for over half an hour since Si had put a pint down in front of his friend and said, 'She's gone. They said there were unexpected complications with the infection. Three o'clock this morning.'

'Why the bloody hell are you at work then?' Adam had gasped. 'Where are Tess and Joe?'

'They're with my mum. Haven't told them yet. Haven't told anyone yet.'

Adam was silent.

'They called me at ten past three, so I didn't even get to see her. They said she wasn't in pain. I don't know what to...'

Adam stared awkwardly into his pint, not knowing what else to say. Si and Shubu had two children – Tess, a volatile thirteen-year-old, and nine-year-old Joe.

Si picked up his beer and downed it in one. He wanted to talk about Shubu, but every time he had tried to speak, the words had stuck in his throat. 'Better get home now,' he said. 'Tess has a dance exam in the morning and I don't know what she needs. Shubu...' Si stood up to leave. He looked washed out. The dark circles under his eyes made him appear ghostly. Forcing down the burning lump from his throat he mumbled as he turned to leave, 'See ya. Might not be in tomorrow.'

Adam rose, almost knocking over his glass, calling to Si's back, 'You better bloody not be. I'll call you. Dinks and I'll have the kids. Anytime... You know, any time.'

'Yeah, thanks.' Si's words were flat and empty and he did not turn round.

As Si walked home, he was numb and felt nothing but a dull, heavy emptiness inside, his head thumping. Why? Why? Why? he asked himself, over and over. The power of grief and confusion was overwhelming. What had gone wrong? He needed to gain clarity and to understand.

Adam walked slowly down the narrow lane lined by overhanging trees, the leaves were wet underfoot. He breathed in the smell of chimney smoke from neighbouring houses. Everything was still, except for the occasional hoot of an owl and the dull rumbling of motorway traffic a distance away.

He sat on a bench in the park, thinking about Si, tears springing up in his eyes, his chest tight. He thought about what he would do if Darinka died, how he would manage with the kids. He wondered how Tess would cope without her mum to guide her. As he remembered his own mum he let out a gasp.

The moon was full, casting a ghostly shadow across the grass. A shiver ran down his neck. As he breathed deeply, he closed his eyes, wishing like a child, that he was more capable of dealing with his emotions.

Suddenly, when he heard steps close by, he opened his eyes wide and his heart began to pound.

'Ah now, they say our dead are never dead to us, until we've forgotten them. I think that's true, don't you?'

'Shit!' Adam jumped up, alarmed, until he realised who it was. 'Sorry! You scared the...'

Dorothy stood next to him, speaking gently. 'Do you want to be alone, pet?'

'No, no... Don't go. No...I...No, you just surprised me, that's all.' Adam shocked himself at the urgency of his response, how relieved he was to see her.

'Well then, let me share this poem I learnt as a child, which has helped me through many sorrows.' She sat down and nodded for him to join her.

How could she possibly know about Shubu? Adam wondered, confused.

She continued quietly, her voice soothing:

Do not stand at my grave and weep
I am not there. I do not sleep.
I am a thousand winds that blow.
I am the diamond glints on snow.
I am the sunlight on ripened grain.

I am the gentle autumn's rain.
When you awaken in the morning's hush
I am the swift, uplifting rush
Of quiet birds in circled flight.
I am the soft stars that shine at night.
Do not stand at my grave and cry
I am not there. I did not die.

'Wise words from Clare Harner, pet. Sometimes when we feel the grief of someone moving on from us, stories can help. Do you remember telling me that you weren't very good at making up stories and when you were young you just wanted to be outside?'

Adam nodded.

'And I suggested that these adventures could form great stories for your children.'

Adam nodded again, sniffing and nervously cracking his knuckles one by one. 'Tommy's always asking me to share stories about my childhood.'

'I bet he is. You're passing on your family knowledge and traditions, connecting him to his past and connecting you to your future,' said Dorothy.

Adam hadn't thought of it this way. 'I'm amazed that he wants me to tell the same story over and over again, asking more questions each time.'

Dorothy laughed. 'Stories of the olden days are exotic aren't they? Characters from your childhood can really enliven your tales. Did you like hearing stories of your mum when she was dancing?'

Instantly multiple memories flooded his brain.

Dorothy continued, 'Well, these stories of your childhood, of your memories, could be helpful to share with your friend now. You want to support him but don't know how. Perhaps you could use these shared memories?'

Adam flashed back to when he and Si were about nine. They were staying with Si's Granny, who lived in a big house in Shipley. It was a time when they had loved building dens and climbing trees in her garden. On one occasion they had discovered a wasp's nest and had started to swat them using large leaves... As they dodged the wasps, they became increasingly smug until Si swatted a huge one directly at Adam. The shock of the sting on his cheek had brought the game to an abrupt end. He'd yelled out in pain, cursing, whilst Si had burst out laughing.

Adam could think of many stories like this one, but how would sharing them help Si? And how could he mention them without it seeming weird?

'Sometimes you just have to trust the story,' said Dorothy. 'Tapping into your own biography and memory is my third secret, pet. I think it might help you all now.' Dorothy had taken some knitting out of her old carpet bag and the needles steadily clicked in a soothing rhythm, like a clock in the night. She continued, 'Our family memories are powerful. We're afraid to speak about death, particularly with children. But, pet, the fact is that their beautiful mum has died and if we don't speak about it, or at least open the door for them to speak about it, then they're likely to take our lead and stay silent. This doesn't remove the pain of their loss; it only sends the hurt underground. Whilst it may not be easy to revisit memories, they will help us to heal, slowly—slowly.'

Dorothy continued to speak about the importance of stories at times of tragedy, grief or trauma.

'They help us to make sense of what's happened. To find a way out of our confusion and towards hope. Stories help us to recognise we're not alone.'

She paused, coughing a little, and bent down to her bag to take out her tin of mints, offering one to Adam who enjoyed the cool, sharp burst of menthol in his mouth.

'Of course, everyone's grief is different. We can never presume to know how it is for another. Some people might not want to speak, whilst others may long to do so. What a story can offer is the space and time to be together, to remember and share. In the same way as hearing Shubu's name will help to keep her memory alive, so telling stories of her life, both before and after Tess and Joe were born, will help them to keep their connection with their mum.'

While this seemed logical to Adam, he was afraid that if he spoke Shubu's name he would cause them to cry. The wind blew through the trees as they heard the hoot of the owl behind the church. He breathed heavily, taking in the smell of smoke from the chimneys of the houses close by.

Once again Dorothy had an uncanny way of pre-empting his concerns. 'Tears are the way for us to release the pain,' she said. 'We're so afraid of tears in our culture and yet how often do we feel better... more refreshed, once we've had the opportunity to really cry? They're all likely to experience a tsunami of emotions whether you speak Shubu's name or not. It's much healthier that these emotions have an outlet.'

The old woman recommended that he, or Si, share the dangers, mistakes or scrapes they'd got into, with Tess. 'She's more likely to share the challenges she's facing if she hears the stuff you were up to at a similar age!'

Adam chuckled, as Dorothy continued.

'Share tales about eruptions, such as volcanos, hurricanes or the overthrow of leaders, with her now that she's a teenager. She's experiencing her own explosions and outbreaks both internally and externally and of course, she's facing additional confusions, poor love.'

Although he felt inadequate for the task, he decided he would mention the wasp story to Si. He slowly cracked his knuckles as he wondered how Si would respond. Maybe he would share some of Dorothy's suggestions with him.

Si and Shubu lived in the next road to them, so over the years they had regularly walked the kids to school together.

Dorothy interrupted his thoughts. 'Sometimes, when you're walking side by side it's easier to speak about difficult matters. Maybe Darinka and you could take Tess and Joe on one of your canal walks? They might enjoy helping with the children and you could share a story or two about Shubu?'

She gave Adam numerous ideas for him to help his mate. 'Memories are moulded and remoulded like clay. You could retell a biographical story, which you share with them to create a ritual... for example, the night before Shubu's birthday perhaps? Or at Christmas?'

Adam told her the two families traditionally spent New Year together. He thought this would be the perfect opportunity to do something which they could share year after year. However, he worried that it would be too painful for them to get together without Shubu this year.

'People often avoid those who are grieving, out of embarrassment or not knowing what to say. This leaves them much lonelier and more isolated than they might otherwise want. Both you and Si have lived in this village all your lives, so you have an abundant seam of stories all around you. Share the places you hid, where you played, what New Park Primary looked like when you were there. Even what Mr Nicols sold in his sweetie shop.'

Dorothy paused, leaning down into her bag again, this time to pull out a new ball of wool. Apart from an occasional gust of wind which rattled through the trees, all was still.

'Since your house is the one you grew up in, I'm sure Tommy would love to know how it's all changed. It's the same for Si. Does he tell Tess and Joe about the village when you were young?'

Adam didn't know the answer. He realised that although he and Si had known each other all their lives, played football together, discussed work, money, films, went out together on their own and with their families, they rarely spoke about personal matters, about their feelings or about their past.

The deep chime of the church clock cut through the air. It was midnight.

'Using memories works for storytelling in many ways, not just when you're dealing with grief,' advised Dorothy. 'Try starting a story with something factual and then taking it into the realm of imagination. For example, if I tap into a memory of when I was your age, running furiously down Tupp Hill, my open coat flapping behind me, the icy cold wind catching my breath, tearing through my hair, nipping at my cheek and drawing tears up into my eyes, and I use this description in a story it will make the tale so much more vivid.'

The night air was cold on Adam's face. Dorothy swept away strands of hair from across her face as she described her memory.

'Ah, if only these bones would let me run like that now, pet!' Dorothy laughed deeply and mischievously, shaking her head. 'But these memories will make your stories richer, and as you describe them pictures will form in the children's minds.'

'Marija prefers stories that are factual,' said Adam. 'When I told her about my sister scaring me in the dark it seemed to help her. I think she's a bit afraid of the dark.'

Dorothy suggested that if he shared any memories of finding his way through the darkness or even when he enjoyed it, for example playing Murder in the Dark, this could further dispel her fears.

'And you're suggesting I combine some of my memories with something I make up?' asked Adam.

'Oh yes, pet, what a marvellous way to create a story.'

The moon had slipped behind a cloud and the owl hooted in the trees behind the church. Adam was cold and a shiver shot through his body. He stood up, stretched his arms above his head and stamped his feet to warm them. Dorothy seemed impervious to the cold.

She was silent until he sat down again, her needles continuing to click out a steady rhythm.

'How about playing 'Pass the Boot' with Tess and Joe and with Tommy too?' she asked.

Adam looked at her quizzically.

'Well, write out a series of random words on pieces of paper, fold them individually and pop them into a container. I use an old boot. Words like owl, holiday, eggs, bonfire, picnic, scarf, blackberries, swim, moon...'

Dorothy put her knitting down for a moment to rearrange her shawl and push back her hair. 'So, now, where was I? Oh yes, put your words in and then take turns to pick out a word to use it as the stimulus to tell a short story from a memory.

'The next person then picks out a new word. You can either tell individual stories or you could make up one continuous story between you. If you want to play with Marija and Luka, you could use pictures or colours instead of words.'

Adam wanted to give it a go but decided that he would try it with his own kids before seeing if Tess and Joe wanted to play, afraid that they would both find it too babyish.

'So, remember my secrets to create your stories. Strengthen your imagination, tap into your senses, use your observation skills and now you can add in your memories. These are my fundamental three pillars for creating splendid spontaneous stories!' Dorothy laughed, not taking herself too seriously.

He heard her but, sitting in the darkness, he couldn't help but feel spooked that Dorothy knew so

much about his family and about Si and Shubu too. He
didn't know anything about her. Had she always lived
in the village without him knowing? Darinka seemed
to think she had been the local midwife, but no one
they asked had heard anything about her.

Adam was so caught up in these thoughts he
hadn't noticed that the clicking of the needles had
ceased. Dorothy was gone. He knew it was pointless
trying to see where. He sat for a while longer, breathing
deeply and considering how he would break the news
of Shubu to Darinka, if she didn't already know.

He walked slowly up the hill to their old mill worker's
cottage, which had been his childhood home. Over the
years Darinka and he had made changes to the house,
including a two-storey extension at the back, to make
space for an upstairs bathroom and third bedroom.
Downstairs they'd added a pantry behind the kitchen
and of course the Squidge Room off the sitting room.
He had never wanted to repaint the lime green door,
which his mum had painted when he was a child. It
was her favourite colour. Now he opened and closed
it as quietly as he could. The warmth of the room was
striking and he could see the flickering glow of the
embers in the fire grate.

Without turning the lights on, he headed for the stairs.
When Darinka spoke, he nearly jumped out of his skin.

'How's Si?' Darinka was curled up under the red
blanket on the sofa in front of the fire. Her face was tear
-stained and her eyes swollen.

'Oh! I thought you'd be asleep, sorry sweetie.'

She'd waited up for him, although she had been nodding off when she heard the front door and felt the rush of cold night air blow through the room.

He sat next to her, took her hand and kissed her tenderly. 'You've heard?' he said to her in a whisper.

She nodded, holding back more tears. 'Let's not talk about it tonight,' she said. 'It's too horrible to think about.'

'It's a shock, isn't it? I can't believe it to be honest.' Adam held Darinka's hand, stroking it gently. 'Ok, let's talk another time.' They sat in silence for a while. Adam was staring into space.

Darinka squeezed his hand and leant forward to kiss him. 'What are you thinking about?'

'Dinks, do you remember playing that game of charades? It was Shubu's turn and she tried to describe that play you'd seen in York?'

Darinka laughed out loud, holding her hand up to her mouth. 'Oh, that was hilarious! She was so funny, falling on the floor, jumping up and down, pointing wildly at me. I just couldn't get it. I think we'd all had way too much to drink, hadn't we?' Darinka smiled, tears falling freely down her flushed cheeks. They reminisced about that particular evening, filling in the details between them.

When eventually they fell silent again Darinka's eyes dropped as she remembered. The sitting room was cold. She rubbed her eyes and sniffed. 'I can't bear that she's gone, Adam. She was the glue. I loved how fierce she was, about just about everything.' Darinka let out a deep breath and blew her nose noisily.

Adam chuckled at the sound. 'It makes me so relieved that you're here, next to me, healthy and well.'

She looked deeply into his sad eyes. 'You're cold. Have you been with Si all this time?' She gave him a section of the blanket to put across his knees.

'No, I was in the churchyard. Guess what? Dorothy joined me, out of nowhere. She freaked me out, but to be fair I was actually pleased to see her.'

Darinka sat up, suddenly more awake, asking questions.

'I'm exhausted, but I'll try to remember as much as I can,' said Adam. 'She talked mostly about personal stories.'

'Is that why you asked me about Shubu and the charades?'

Adam nodded. 'I didn't intend to, but then I thought about what Dorothy said, that memories, and stories, help us to process things that we find difficult to handle. The memory of that night with Shubu was so vivid, I wondered if it was for you too. We all had so much fun, didn't we?'

'Yes.' Darinka smiled softly. 'It was lovely to think about her when she was well and not just about the fact that she's gone.'

Darinka had more questions and he answered with something else Dorothy had said, 'Sometimes delving into memories can be painful, tender, raw, so she said to be gentle with ourselves if this happened. She said it would be good to share our memories with the kids.'

Darinka thought about it and slowly began to tease out her own thoughts. 'It makes so much sense to share stories with them about our own families, our ancestors, us when we were young. Tonight, I was telling Marija and Luka a story about one of those plants he brought in from our walk the other day. Marija was being stroppy cos she wasn't interested. She likes to hear stories about people. I gave up and Luka started crying. I wonder if I'd combined those two elements it would have kept them both happy. Could have prevented a meltdown, eh?'

Darinka giggled and pulled Adam under the blanket with her, he was still so cold and damp, she wrapped her legs round him to help warm him. 'Adam, what else did she tell you?'

'She said that I should think of stories from the whole of my life, you know – me backpacking, meeting you, stuff like that.' Adam hesitated, his eyes dropped as he felt them spike with tears. 'Dinks, it made me realise how much you gave up to be with me.'

They were both quiet. Darinka felt safe, wrapped in Adam's arms. She nuzzled her head into his chest, breathing in his smell and listening to his heartbeat. Her eyes, puffy from crying, closed as she drifted in and out of sleep. Adam was gazing at her and stroking her hair, never wanting to forget this moment.

After a while she shook herself awake, pleading with him to continue.

'OK, OK. So, Dorothy said that if we use our memories to sprinkle into stories, it will enhance the tale. Dinks, she was adamant that you should tell the kids stories in Slovene, or at least pepper them with words and phrases... sing childhood songs, that kind of thing. I like that idea. Let's dig out some of your old photo albums. It'd be great if the kids were bilingual, wouldn't it?' Adam added sleepily, 'Dorothy reminds me a bit of Irena.'

'Yes, I've thought that too.' Darinka smiled softly. She missed her mum, Irena, very much. Their family home was in Gabrovka, about an hour's drive east of the capital, Ljubljana, and most of Darinka's aunts, uncles, cousins and siblings still lived in close proximity.

Irena was anxious about travelling and, since she had to sleep on the sofa in the sitting room when she came to stay, she hadn't visited more than a couple of times in the past four years. When Darinka ever mentioned booking a holiday in Slovenia, Adam somehow found a way out of it. Even though he had met Darinka whilst travelling there, he said he felt awkward with her large, noisy family and was out of his depth, unable to understand the conversations. Darinka regularly spoke with her mum on the phone although Irena would not use a mobile. During these conversations Darinka tried to explain, 'Mama, we're busy here. I promise, when the twins are a little older, I'll bring them and stay for a whole month!' Irena accepted it was too much for her daughter to bring three tiny children on a plane on her own.

'I miss my grandchildren,' Irena would say at the end of every call. 'Darinka why are you so far away? How can I be a good *Babica* to them when I don't see them?' It made Darinka less inclined to call as she couldn't bear her mother's pain.

Adam and she talked well into the night and they agreed to try the Pass the Boot game after school tomorrow. When eventually they climbed into bed, Adam remembered something else Dorothy had said. 'She said that when we put the children to bed, we could try telling them the story of their day.'

'I do this already.' Darinka yawned, pleased with herself.

'She suggested that we tell it in reverse order. Apparently, it's a good way for them to process the facts and help them get to sleep.' He leant across to kiss her. 'Dinks, shall we go and visit your mum in the holidays?'

Darinka, shattered from the news about Shubu, could hardly take this in. She lay in the dark, her heart beating fast, tears rolling down her face, trying to balance the contradiction between devastation and elation.

Adam was asleep before Darinka replied, 'Yes, yes, yes. *Ljubim te*, sweetie.'

There was silence. In less than an hour the dawn chorus would begin.

Story Games from Chapter 3

Pass the Boot Game – see page 100

For three or more players

- Write a series of unrelated words on separate pieces of paper, for example: beach, hair dryer, cat, library, bonfire, chocolate cake.
- Fold up each scrap of paper and place them into a container, such as a hat, bag or boot.
- Each player takes it in turns to pick out a word which might trigger a memory.
- Tell the story which can be the memory itself or inspired by it.
- Take it in turns to tell your short story.
- If two or more players remember the same memory, let them tell the story from their own perspective. This is a great way to understand that there is always more than one side to every story.

If you're playing this game with young children, draw pictures on the pieces of paper instead of words.

Pass the Boot Scrapbook

- Paste all the words from the game into a scrapbook to look back through at the end of the year. Additionally, alongside some of the words you could write the story prompted by this word. In this way you are keeping a record of your story memories which you create together.

Did you know?

- Telling the story of your day in reverse order isn't only soothing but also beneficial. A recent study at the University of Birmingham concluded that when we remember a past event the human brain reconstructs that experience in reverse order. Additionally, researchers at Korea University Business School ran a series of studies which found that those people who planned backwards performed better than those who planned forward.

- Memory and the Senses are very closely aligned. Smell is the only fully developed sense a foetus has in the womb! It is the sense that is most developed in a child up until around ten years-old when sight takes over. Smell and emotion are stored as one memory, so childhood tends to be the period in which we create the basis for smells we will like and those we will hate for the rest of our lives.

Further reading...

The Year of Magical Thinking, by Joan Didion.

Grief Is the Thing with Feathers, by Max Porter.

Sad Book, by Michael Rosen.

Grief Works: Stories of Life, Death and Surviving, by Julia Samuel.

CHAPTER 4

In Search of Treasure
The Fourth Secret – Puppets and Props

'I could never be on stage on my own.
But puppets can say things that humans can't say.'
Nina Conti

'Let's go to Mrs Oddie's Farm tomorrow,' Adam suggested to Darinka after they'd put the children to bed. 'I'll drop you off and then take Tommy for his hair cut. I could do with one too.'

'Not tomorrow sweetie. Rachel has asked if we can have Lucy for the day.'

'We can take her with us.' Adam was determined. Darinka's birthday was on Tuesday, five weeks to the day since Shubu died. He hadn't found a present for her, so he wanted to take Tommy with him to help choose something really special. Darinka sighed heavily, shaking her head, knowing how futile it was to argue when Adam got an idea stuck in his head. He was so persuasive. She took hold of his hand and led him towards the sofa.

'Okay, I'll text Rachel, see what she says. Now, let's watch a film.'

Lucy, their niece, was only a few months younger than Tommy and they played well together.

Rachel had suspected something was different about her daughter when she was around six months old but wasn't sure. She had confided in Darinka as David, Lucy's dad, was convinced that Rachel was fussing over nothing.

'Lucy just won't touch the food I put in front of her, or put it in her mouth. She just pushes it on the floor. I'm so worried. Did Tommy do that?' Rachel had asked when she was weaning her daughter.

Another time, Rachel had noticed that Lucy wouldn't stand or sit on the grass, always wanting to be on a mat. She had screamed and screamed when Adam had tried to lift her into a swing in the park, not stopping until he took her out again.

When Darinka and Adam woke the next morning there was a blanket of frost on the roof.

'It's a great day for Mrs Oddie's, isn't it kids?' Adam said with a grin, as the children landed on their bed.

'Yes, Dada, yes,' they screamed, jumping up and down and making the windows rattle.

Darinka raised her eyes to the ceiling, smiled and shook her head. Adam leant over, squeezed her hand and kissed her cheek.

Oddie's was a child-friendly farm and a wonderful, safe place to take the children. Adam's nan and Mrs Oddie had gone to school together. Her farm had been developed over the years and now there were a wide variety of activities, inside and out, for all the family. Tommy loved climbing over and under the straw bales, Luka wanted to feed the animals, particularly the pygmy goats, whilst Marija gravitated towards the sand and water, panning for gold and gems in Blackbeard's Bay, pretending to be a pirate.

Adam smiled. 'It's much better at this time of year, Dinks, there's hardly anyone there.'

'Mmm,' she replied. 'But you're not going to be the one sitting out in the cold, are you?'

'Tommy, we're going to get our hair cut, how does that sound, mate?'

Tommy threw his arms round his dad's neck, beaming. He stuck his tongue out cheekily at his brother and sister. 'I'm going on my own with Dada.'

Marija stuck her tongue out in response.

A text from Rachel confirmed Adam's plan.

Lucy up for going to Farm :) She knows T isn't going. Will drop off at 9.30, Rxx

'Lucy's looking forward to the farm, aren't you, Lou?' Rachel gave Darinka a hug and handed over wellies, gloves and a hat. 'It'll give me a chance to get some work done. I'm so behind.'

She bent down to give her daughter a kiss, sweeping her hair out of her mouth.

'Stop chewing it rascal! Remember, Tommy's going with Uncle Adam into town for his haircut, so he won't be at the farm.'

Lucy nodded. 'I know that.'

Rachel thanked Darinka again and hugged her

brother. 'Text me when you're back and I'll come and collect her. Thanks both. Be good, Lou.'

As Adam loaded everything into the boot, Lucy and Tommy were whispering conspiratorially in the back of the car.

Since first meeting Dorothy, over three months ago, Darinka and Adam had started to play games in the car with the children, particularly at the start of any trip. It made travelling more fun and Darinka had noticed that once they'd played for a while the children continued with their own games, leaving her and Adam free to chat. Sometimes they played the ABC or the Cloud game.

Tommy turned to Lucy and said, 'Want to play I -Spy?'

Fifteen minutes later they arrived at Oddie's. Darinka helped Marija and Luka out of their booster seats, pleased there weren't many other cars in the car park. Large crowds and loud noise were difficult for Lucy to deal with and she was nervous around children she didn't know, so the fewer people the better.

'*Dragi moj*, see you later. We'll meet you back here. Text me,' Darinka said.

Tommy joined his dad in the front and they waved goodbye.

The three children followed Darinka through the barrier, Lucy and Marija holding hands. Luka excitedly marched towards the goats. Darinka had bought them each a bag of feed.

'Will you hold mine, Aunty Dinks?' asked Lucy, who didn't like to touch the brown paper bag.

As they made their way across the forecourt, Lucy told Marija, 'It's not a cage, it's a loafing shed.'

Marija looked up to her cousin, smiling and asked, 'Loping shed?'

'LoaFing… like a loaf of bread.'

Marija nodded.

After a short time with the goats, Luka handed his mum his empty bag of feed, pulling on her coat sleeve, and banging her hand. 'Mama, let's go see the pigs – Mama?'

Marija was about to cry out when Darinka interjected, 'Let's see what stories we can make in the sandpit, on our way to the pigs.' This satisfied them all.

The sand was heavy and damp and there was no one else around. Darinka wanted the children to be outside whilst there was still some light, even though she was shivering. She plunged her hands deep into her anorak pockets, annoyed with herself for leaving her hat and gloves in the car.

Marija and Luka threw off their mittens and dived straight into the sand, building up shapes and objects. Lucy didn't want to touch the gritty, sticky sand.

Darinka, who was the youngest of five, had loved making huge sandcastles on the beach with her siblings. Her mum always said, 'Sand's meant to be swept away, make it and let it go.' but Lucy became anxious every time the twins gleefully smashed what they'd built.

Darinka remembered the last time she and Rachel had come together. Unusually, Lucy had sat in the pit, although close to the edge, carefully building a castle. Unfortunately, as Tommy ran to get his drink, he had inadvertently knocked it over. She had burst into tears and refused to go back in. Today, Lucy sat next to her aunty calling out to the twins, telling them what to do.

Suddenly Marija called out, 'Let's go to Beardy-Bear, Mama.'

Darinka laughed, nodding assent. 'Okay! Blackbeard's Bay. Good idea. Luce, we'll have a few more minutes here and then we'll go over there, OK?' She pointed down the hill, across to the bottom field where a huge wooden structure was clearly visible.

Lucy nodded. She knew the farm well, but still she took time to adjust to change, however small and insignificant. Darinka knew to give her processing time. Only a couple of weeks ago, Tommy had gone to Lucy's house after school and as they played a game of Snap he changed the rules and Lucy started sobbing, clinging to her mum and refusing to let go. When Darinka picked Tommy up, she asked him what had happened.

'Nothing really,' he'd said casually. 'She was just being Lucy.'

Blackbeard's Bay was the gold panning area and Marija's favourite spot. Darinka asked Lucy if she would like to go ahead with the twins while she gathered their bags.

'I can do that, Aunty Dinks,' Lucy said in a grown -up way. 'Hold my hands, Luka, Marija.'

Marija threw off her hat. 'Too hot,' she declared. Luka copied.

Darinka's joints were stiffening in the damp November air. She wished she'd brought an extra jumper and considered wearing the children's mittens on the ends of her fingers.

Luka had forgotten all about the pigs. When Darinka joined them, Lucy was already instructing him how to fill his pan with sand from the bottom of the water trough. She was humming to herself, as she often did.

Darinka helped them to sift through the sand to see what shining treasures they could find.

Luka yelled out when they spotted a large, shiny gold nugget. Marija, who was using her fingers as a sieve, stopped.

'That's big,' she said admiringly, urged on to search for her own.

The sound of screeching geese in formation, black against the grey-white sky, caught their attention for a moment as Darinka walked over to sit on the bench a few metres away. She put down the bags and pulled her jacket tight around her. Before she looked up she heard the soothing and familiar voice.

'Is this seat taken, pet?' A smiling, weather-worn face, reddy-grey hair piled up in a messy knot and the distinctive pink and orange shawl. Dorothy grinned, her eyes dancing. 'Hello, how are you all?'

Darinka laughed. 'Oh! Hello. I'm cold, but the kids are all good!' She shuffled her bags off the bench like an excited schoolgirl, her mind racing. How did Dorothy manage to appear out of nowhere? She was cross that Rachel wasn't there and wondered if Adam and Tommy would get to see her later. Maybe Dorothy could give her ideas about stories for Lucy. She would explain about her niece...

The two women sat side by side, watching the children.

'How lovely to see Lucy. How is she?' Dorothy asked.

Darinka dived into the middle of her thoughts, not noticing that Dorothy knew Lucy's name.

'I didn't know this, but apparently the speech and language therapist told Rachel that girls are less likely to get diagnosed with autism spectrum disorder, because their symptoms are different from boys, and are more likely to mask any signs. She said that's cos girls often want to be more sociable.'

Dorothy nodded thoughtfully. 'Mmm, interesting,' she said. 'You've reminded me of one of my granddaughters who was diagnosed with Asperger's, back in the early days of the research. She was misdiagnosed several times and it was a struggle for her parents to get the support they needed. But, when it came, the diagnosis helped them, not least to understand her better. My granddaughter's all grown up now, working as part of the forensics team for a large accountancy firm.'

Darinka, absorbed in her own thoughts, blurted out, 'How can stories help Lucy?'

Dorothy considered the question, laughing. 'Gosh, well, you do like to challenge me with your questions, don't you?' She paused, looking up as a plane cast white lines across the sky, considering the question for a moment.

'My first thought is that the tales we spin have a powerful impact on any child, particularly how they view themselves in the world. So, well-crafted stories could help Lucy to feel less alone in the world – more understood and more valued. They might also help her to process situations and events that she encounters in her day-to-day life.'

Dorothy took her small tin of mints from her

pocket and, offering one to Darinka, took one for herself. She sat, watching the children play, thinking before she continued.

'You could use tales as a bridge when she seems distant or disconnected. Importantly, using stories, songs or rhymes as part of a steady, repetitive rhythm across her day will make her feel more secure and safe.' Dorothy drew her shawl a little closer around her and, rummaging in her bag, brought out a pair of woollen gloves. 'Here, I've got a second pair, if you'd like to wear them?'

Darinka was grateful for the dark blue woollen gloves, which she slipped on before rubbing her hands vigorously to warm them. She had known that Dorothy would have ideas she could share with Rachel.

'My fourth secret explores the use of puppets and props in storytelling. Using well-chosen props can be as therapeutic as they are magical,' Dorothy said. 'Did you know that puppetry, which is the use of a prop to tell a story, has potentially been around for over 5,000 years? Any object big or small, from nature or your house, can be used as a prompt to inspire a story. It's fun to share a story – like the ABC Story game – using a prop.'

Darinka had bought Tommy a set of finger puppets last Christmas, but he hadn't shown any interest in them. She remembered being disappointed, not least because she wanted to experiment with them. When Darinka mentioned this, Dorothy asked, 'Has he ever seen anyone using finger puppets before?'

Darinka shook her head. 'Not to my knowledge.'

'You need to bring them to life for him if you want

to spark his interest. But you'll also need to play with them more than once, make a connection with them yourself. Of course, there's always the chance that he still doesn't like them, but you won't know that unless you try!'

Darinka decided to search for them. They were probably in one of the toy boxes in the Squidge Room. She'd ask Tommy if he knew where they were.

'It seems to me,' Dorothy continued, 'that more important than anything is that we accept each child. Love them for who they are, not what we want them to be. Not an easy thing to do, by any means. In my experience it takes a great deal of courage and humility, but we can keep that as our intention, learning as we go.'

She sighed and then, with a twinkle in her eye, said, 'Oh! I remember desperately wanting my children to play the piano. They hated their lessons and wouldn't practice. When eventually I realised that it was me who wanted to play, I took their lessons for myself. I didn't nag at them anymore because I loved playing. Ironically, after a while two of them started to play again! Perhaps it's the same with finger puppets?'

The women burst into peals of laughter and Darinka nodded in agreement. This noise brought Luka running over to see what was happening. He hid behind his mum, staring at Dorothy who gave the little boy a cheeky wink.

'You remember Dotty, don't you?' said Darinka, putting her arm around her son. Tommy often asked for a 'Dotty story' or game and Dorothy's name had been mentioned many times since their windmill encounter.

'Hello pet,' said Dotty.

He stepped towards her, his thumb in his mouth.

'Looks like you're finding pirate treasure, Captain Luka.'

This made him giggle and he ran to collect his golden treasure to show Dorothy.

'Thank you, kind sir.' Dotty took the nugget from him with great care.

Marija, wet from head to toe, looked sternly at Dorothy as she stood next to Luka and said, 'You're Dotty, aren't you?'

'Yes, pet, I am.' She smiled and winked at the girl.

Marija held out her hand, revealing her gems and stones.

Although Lucy was curious, she stayed at a safe distance. Darinka was anxious to explain to her niece who this new person was. Dorothy assured her that Lucy would come closer in her own time, once she had had time to observe for a while.

Dorothy took a large cream silk handkerchief from her pocket, inviting the twins to lay down their valuable objects on it. Her voice dropped to a whisper and she said, 'Let's keep these safely in my Story Bag, who knows what stories might emerge!'

With the exception of one small blue gemstone, Dorothy gathered the objects up into her hanky, which she twisted closed. She asked the twins to suggest the name of an animal.

'Bunny,' said Marija immediately, having seen a couple over by the bushes.

'Bushy,' said Luka almost simultaneously.

'Ah! Yes, Bushy Bunny,' the woman confirmed, to

the delight of both children. Dorothy held up the blue stone. 'And did you know that Bushy used this small gemstone to make a special radio to send messages from the tree elves to the root gnomes?'

Marija and Luka stared at her, open-mouthed as she continued, conspiratorially.

'Where does Bushy live?' she asked the twins.

'By that tree.' Luka pointed to the cluster of trees at the back of the panning area.

Dorothy nodded. As she continued the story, Lucy slowly crept closer, chewing on her hair nervously, not knowing what was going to happen next in the story. She continued to listen, eyes wide, as Dorothy's quiet voice drew her in.

Dorothy wove a tale about Bunny, North Wind and the Great Old Oak. When she brought the tale to an end, Marija gently took the blue stone from out of the Wise Woman's hand and placed it down under the nearest tree, patting it softly as she whispered to it, 'I leave it for Bushy to collect.'

Darinka blinked, realising she'd been completely lost in the story.

'How do you know if the rabbit will find it?' asked Lucy urgently.

'Mmm, that's a good question. Do you think Bushy will find it?'

Lucy nodded, adding, 'But Luka and Marija should keep the rest of the treasure to take home, shouldn't they?'

'Ah yes, definitely.' Dorothy held out her cream handkerchief filled with the stones the twins had collected. 'This Story Bag holds lots of story treasures. Maybe they'll share some with you for helping them?'

'Yes, one for you,' said Marija, taking the hanky out of Dorothy's hand.

Dorothy winked at Darinka and gestured for her to look over at Lucy who was staring at the various rocks on the handkerchief, deciding whether to take one or not.

Darinka could see that this Wise Woman's kind and gentle manner was rubbing off on them all. She chuckled to herself, conscious that she was copying Dorothy's tone and gestures at home. At the same time, she was also aware that listening to Dorothy made her feel that she wasn't as good a mum as she could be.

'Let's find more!' Luka grabbed Marija and pulled her away from the women towards the water. Lucy followed. Dorothy leant over and touched Darinka's arm softly.

'You're doing a great job as a mum, you know, pet.'

Darinka, caught off guard by these words, felt a thump in her chest as a tear rose in her eye. She put her hand to her heart, rubbing slowly.

'Thanks,' she said in a tiny voice, coughing uncomfortably, before containing herself, 'but did you... did you just make up that story?'

'Yes, pet,' she laughed. 'It's not so difficult when you use three elements that you find in all stories – Person, Obstacle and Place. If you use each of these as stepping-stones it will make it much easier for you to make up stories with the children. I call them my 'POP Stories'. The Person could be a puppet, an animal or creature. The Obstacle could be a quest, a villain or an object, one that you have to hand, or that the children find, like when we were in the woods that time. The Place sets your scene, the landscape, which could be a geographical area or – as one of my children suggested – '*The belly of a whale!*'. Then you POP them all together to make up a story!'

Darinka stamped her feet which had gone numb from the cold. She breathed deeply, thinking about how easy Dorothy made it seem, and making a pact with herself that she would see if she could come up with a 'POP Story' instead of reading a book with the children at bedtime.

Dorothy rubbed the side of her face brusquely and finished her explanation. 'As you heard, I used these ingredients in my story with Bushy Bunny, the blue gemstone and the old oak tree. Of course, Brother North Wind, our villain, provides the tension, which makes the story more interesting. 'POP Stories' can be used in so many ways. There is an endless stream of story, pet.'

'I'm hungry,' Lucy said as she ran towards the bench.

'Oh! *Oprosti*, Luce.' Darinka hadn't noticed the time. She scrambled in her bag, muttering, cross with herself that Lucy had to remind her.

When the sandwiches, carrot strips, crisps and juice were laid out on the bench she gestured to Lucy and said, 'Here, help yourself *sonček moj*. Luka, Marija, lunchtime!'

Luka ran straight over, wiping his hands on his coat and grabbing a cheese sandwich.

Marija, engrossed in her search for gold, ignored her mum until Lucy took her by the hand and guided her back to the bench. Darinka knew Marija would be soaking wet, despite wearing her waterproofs, so was pleased she had put spare clothes in her bag.

After lunch Darinka, whose nose was icy with cold, suggested they head off inside to feed the pigs. As they packed up their things her phone pinged,

Be with you in 30 mins :)

Darinka texted Adam back.

OK. Meet at the entrance when you get here x

She called to the children to let them know that Tommy was on his way.

'Yeah!' they cried out. Lucy took hold of Marija and Luka's hands and led them towards the pigsty, the three of them chatting happily about Bushy Bunny and the special radio.

Darinka and Dorothy walked slowly behind the kids. Dorothy had been silent during lunch, but when Darinka asked her about ideas to help Lucy, she rubbed her fingers across her lips and considered for a moment.

'Well, I wonder if, for Lucy, one special puppet, the same one every time, might help her. It could lend a hand with everyday tasks like cleaning her teeth or doing homework,' Dorothy suggested. 'My granddaughter made a surprising connection with Kika Mouse, one of my glove puppets. When Kika shared any of her feelings, maybe a fear or anxiety, it helped my granddaughter to express her feelings too. If Lucy's having an unsettling day or having trouble navigating sudden changes this puppet, speaking in its own unique way and not with your voice, might be useful.'

Darinka wanted to share this with Rachel, wondering if they already had a puppet at home that she didn't know about.

Dorothy continued, 'A puppet could speak on behalf of a shy child or, as was the case for me, when my children were fed up with listening to me giving them instructions, they were able to listen to our family puppet much more readily. Oh, I did bark out my orders, pet!' Dorothy chuckled, a self-deprecating laugh, shaking her head.

By the time they arrived at the sty the children were ready to move on.

'Let's go to the straw sheds then, before we go home,' Darinka said, turning to Lucy. 'We'll be leaving soon *draga moja*, and then you're coming to our house to play with Tommy until your mum picks you up.'

Marija grabbed Luka's hand and pulled him away from the pigs, one of whom was still snuffling at the ground, grunting and looking for more pellets.

In the large barn the twins immediately dropped their hats and scarves onto the straw bale seats before climbing up the stepped structure. Darinka laid out a rug for Lucy as she didn't like the texture of the straw but wanted to sit next to her aunty. The place was almost empty, so Lucy gladly watched her cousins, shouting out instructions to them from time to time.

Dorothy sat on the other side of Lucy as they chatted together quietly. Luka called out for Lucy's help and the girl immediately ran off to her young cousin. Dorothy dusted down her blue velvet skirt and, pulling strands of hair from her face, asked Darinka for some of their water.

'You make it all sound so simple,' Darinka sighed deeply, in awe of Dorothy, still trying to shake off thoughts of being inadequate.

Dorothy leant over and touched Darinka's gloved hand.

'You really don't have to make it difficult for yourself, pet. You don't have to try to be a super-mum, you know. None of us ever are! I've had a lot of time, a lot of children and believe me, I've made lots of mistakes.'

Darinka smiled reluctantly as Dorothy looked her straight in the eyes and said, 'Listen to me, these things I'm sharing with you are tools to help you, not chains to restrain you or make you feel bad. My grandmother always used to say, "Let the story do the hard work."'

Darinka wanted to ask more but Lucy pulled at her hand. 'I think Marija's tired, Aunty Dinks.'

Darinka called the twins over to her, offering them a drink of water and wrapping her arms around them. Their cheeks were glowing and they were both out of breath having played a game of tag with some of the children who had just arrived.

'Come and sit with me here, *ljubica moja*.' Darinka made space for Marija, between her and Dorothy.

The Wise Woman began to sing softly, one simple verse after another about snowdrops, sleeping caterpillars and Jack Frost. By the end of it, Marija had her head resting on Dorothy's lap, eyes half closed. Lucy leant against Dorothy's shawl and Luka, sucking his thumb, cuddled up at the other side of his mum.

Darinka couldn't believe how relaxed Lucy was with Dorothy. She wanted to take a photo – Rachel would never believe her otherwise.

Dorothy turned to Darinka and whispered, 'What I've learnt over the years is that these simple songs and stories demonstrate to the child that all is well in the world and that there is kindness all around them. From this place of safety, they can grow deep roots to help them move to the next stage of their development.'

It reminded Darinka of her first meeting with Dorothy at the windmill. These quiet, unhurried moments were powerful and healing. Darinka was beginning to appreciate what Dorothy meant when she said that stories helped children to develop and grow. She could see how crucial tales are for language development and for improving the children's powers of concentration but also that stories really could help children to flourish and thrive.

Darinka wasn't sure how long they stayed in this relaxed state, but it was Marija who sat up first.

'When's Dada be here?' she asked.

'Very soon, sweetie.' Darinka picked up her phone as it pinged with a text.

Just parking, xx

'He's here now, *ljubica moja*,' she said, stroking Marija's face.

Darinka sent a voice note, 'See you at the entrance in 5.' as she gathered up their things.

All three children sat up.

'Doesn't take long to restore those batteries does it, pet? Wish mine were the same. Takes me much longer these days!' The two women both laughed.

'Let's go kids.' When Darinka looked up to say how pleased Adam and Tommy would be to see her, the Wise Woman was nowhere to be seen.

Ringing in Darinka's ears was this sentence, 'From the age of three years, children enter a world full of imagination, full of possibilities. If this stage is unhurried, then children develop a life-long urge for learning.'

STORY GAMES FROM CHAPTER 4

I–Spy – see page 114
For two or more players
- The first player picks an object that everyone can see and gives the first letter of the object as a clue. For example, if the player chooses chair, they say, 'I spy with my little eye something beginning with C.'
- Players take it in turns to guess what it might be. The first person to guess the right answer chooses an object for the rest of the players to guess.

POP Stories – see page 123
For two or more players
- Explore each of these three elements: The Person (character, animal, creature, alien), The Obstacle (challenge, villain, object), The Place (landscape, time and space) separately, one by one.
- Create The Person by playing picture consequences. The first player draws the head, passes it unseen (by means of folding) to the second player who draws the body, then on to the third player who draws the legs and feet. The fourth player names The Person. The composite person is then revealed to all by unfolding the paper.
- Create The Obstacle by collecting a small bag of objects (e.g. a stone, keys, sock, ring, acorn, toothbrush etc.). The players each draw out an object, without looking, and describe what it is to the rest of the players. In the description include for example: how old it is, where it might have come from or who it belongs to. This object might be 'more than it first appears to

be'. This object could be lost in the story, or what our character uses to overcome a problem.

· Find, or draw, a map (of the world or a mythical place). Choose one player to be blindfolded and give them a drawing pin to place on the map. This decides The Place where your story is set.

· Once you have each element, POP (Person, Obstacle and Place) them all together to build your spontaneous story.

Did you know?

· Nobody knows when the first puppet shows were performed in Britain, though there is evidence of puppetry dating back at least 600 years. Glove or hand puppets were very portable, making them popular with travelling minstrels and other medieval entertainers.

· In theatre, props (and objects) are anything movable or portable on a stage, distinct from the actors, costumes and scenery. The use of props was first introduced into British theatre in the 13th century. In our digital age there is something special about telling stories using only our words and a few puppets and props.

Further reading...

Puppet Theatre, by Maija Baric.

The Reason I Jump: One boy's voice from the silence of autism, by Naoki Higashida.

Geek Girl, by Holly Smale.

CHAPTER 5

Ah, Snow!
The Fifth Secret – Wonder

'The more I wonder, the more I love.'
Alice Walker, The Color Purple

When Tommy had opened his curtains he'd yelled, 'Wow! Mama, come, come... snow – it's snowing.'

Half an hour later, Tommy scrambled up onto his dad's knee at breakfast. 'It's a snowy day, Dada.'

The flurry of snow added to the blanket of brilliant white covering the trees, houses and cars. It was already over two feet deep in places, having fallen heavily overnight. Outside it was bitterly cold and unsurprisingly Darinka had received a text to confirm that there would be no school today.

The twins, picking up on Tommy's excitement, were jumping up and down on the sofa, holding hands, calling out, 'Snowy day, snowy day.'

Adam sat at the table, slowly drinking his coffee, remembering back to his own childhood snowy days, which felt like stolen treasure. He had hated school, preferring to be outside. Adam breathed out deeply at the memory of running down the steep hill from his home to collect Si, before the two of them headed off to Buttock Hill to spend the day with their mates, sledging and snowball fighting.

Adam tickled Tommy, still sitting on his knee, and announced, 'No school, eh? Well, that settles it – no work either! Let's get the toboggans out, matey.'

Tommy let out an enormous squeal of delight and joined the twins on the sofa.

'Come off, you'll break it,' Darinka called, heading to the kitchen to clear away the breakfast things. 'Let's get ready to go then!'

Eventually, hand in hand, they set off on foot for Buttock Hill, which was already packed with families sledging down or pulling their sledges back up the steep hill.

As they reached the top the snow had stopped falling, and between the heavy cloud cover the sky was a pale blue and the sun cast shafts of light across the landscape. It was now possible for them to see breathtaking views of the white hills and valleys stretching endlessly towards the horizon. Adam squeezed Darinka's shoulders as they paused, staring at the vastness and beauty.

'Come on, Dada,' called Tommy, making his way towards the mound route.

There were several possible snow runs, but Adam liked this route best because of a small hump of earth halfway down the hill. 'If you catch it just right,' he'd told them, giggling like a kid, as they walked towards the meadow, 'your sledge will take off and when you come back down, bam! You'll fly to the bottom of the hill so fast. It's epic!'

Adam held Tommy tightly round his waist as they went down the first time on one toboggan. The two of them focused on perfecting their technique and their determination intensified when, an hour later, Si and Joe joined them.

Darinka had grown up skiing and when it was her turn she hit the mound with accuracy first time and made it to the bottom in record speed, much to the frustration of Si and Adam and the admiration of their kids.

'That was for Shubu,' Darinka called out, holding her arms out high to receive applause!

It was early afternoon before they headed home, exhilarated and rosy cheeked. Marija sat on Adam's shoulders and Luka clung to his mum's neck as she piggybacked him. Tommy ran alongside, chatting non-stop, all the way.

As Darinka helped the children into the dry, warm clothes she had left out over the radiators, Adam got lunch ready.

'This is the best lunch ever, Dada,' Tommy declared. He ate up all his vegetable soup and warm bread roll. Darinka laughed, knowing that he didn't usually like soup.

After lunch Darinka took the twins for a nap. Almost as soon as they lay down, they were both asleep. Darinka lay down on her bed too and closed her eyes.

Adam and Tommy washed up and Adam told his son they were going to his workshop, which he rented in the village, to make a new toboggan together. Tommy's mouth dropped open, staring at his dad in disbelief before running on the spot and clapping his hands.

'Shh mate, don't wake the twinnies,' Adam laughed.

The snowfall continued and school remained closed for two more days, taking them into the weekend. Darinka was thrilled that Adam had come sledging with them each morning and taken Tommy off to the workshop every afternoon. It had felt like a real holiday, with gentle mornings, bumps and bruises, tears, lazy lunches, side-splitting belly laughs, snow fights and silliness.

'What'll we call her then, eh, mate?' Adam asked Tommy on Saturday afternoon, sanding down their toboggan, which was almost finished.

Tommy watched in awe as his dad painted a lightning bolt down one side and printed the word 'LIGHTENING' in capital letters along the other.

'This is the best! This is the best!' Tommy repeated over and over as he pulled the new sledge proudly back up the hill to their home, sharing his prize with his mum and the twins. 'You see this bit here,' he pointed earnestly as Marija and Luka looked at it, 'that's called a knot. This wood is Ash.'

Adam was standing by his son's side. Darinka slid up behind Adam, putting her arms round him. He took her hands in his, turned his head and kissed her.

'I hope this is for his birthday,' she whispered.

'Mmm, not really,' Adam said sheepishly, realising that he should have thought about that. Darinka laughed, gently pushing him sideways. 'It's only a couple of weeks away. It would have been a perfect gift.' She shook her head and squeezed his arm.

Tommy wanted his new toboggan to be hung on his wall. As Adam was putting it up, he thought about who and where his own father might be, if he even knew about Adam. Was he dead or living somewhere with another family? He felt a sharp pain shoot through his chest as it tightened and he swallowed down a boiling lump in his throat.

'Supper's ready.' Darinka's soothing voice cut through his thoughts but his fury and confusion were slow to dissipate, leaving him scratchy throughout the meal. He snapped when Luka pushed his sister.

'Stop hitting now, otherwise I'll hit you,' he'd shouted harshly across the table, at which Luka burst into tears.

As he sat on the side of their bed that evening, he pulled Darinka towards him. 'Sorry I snapped at tea. It makes me so angry when Luka hits Marija.' Darinka kissed him. She hated it when he shouted at the children, but she'd seen that he was making a real effort to control his anger.

'Snow's melting fast now Dinks, that's the last of it for a while I reckon,' Adam continued as they lay together in the dark, his arm around her.

'It's been a great week, thanks sweetie.'

'Yeah, it really has. You okay if I go to check out the new site in the morning? It'll only take me ten minutes to cycle there.' Adam had successfully quoted to be part of the team due to work on the redevelopment of one of the old warehouses along the canal.

Having remained empty for years, planning permission had recently been granted to convert it into swish apartments and work was due to start on Monday. The developer was reputed to pay well and on time and had bought the two adjoining warehouses. Adam hoped to have secure work for a good number of years.

Darinka and he had often talked about finding a plot of land on which to build their own place. This job could mean they would realise their dream sooner than he had hoped.

'Yes, *ljubček moj*, yes.'

Darinka's eyelids began to close. She was still wrapped in Adam's arms and thought back to how different their relationship had been just a few months earlier. Was it Dorothy who had such an impact on their lives? How could stories make this much difference?

The kids slept longer than usual the next morning. Adam slipped out of the house before anyone was awake. As he crept through the sitting room, Nala the cat was curled up by the fire, its embers giving off a soothing warmth. He gave her a stroke and she purred loudly.

The warehouses butted up to the canal tow path, around three miles from the Dale's home. Since the snow was rapidly turning to ice and slush it was safer to walk than cycle. The sun streaked the sky with pink and blue and deep grey as it rose above the horizon, a low mist clung to the water and Adam glimpsed the crescent moon.

He glanced down to check his phone and text Darinka, and as he looked up, shoving his phone in his pocket, he saw Dorothy walking towards him.

She called out, 'Well, now, how are you?'

'Diddlin' okay, actually,' laughed Adam, pleased to see her.

'May I walk with you a while?' she asked as he got closer.

'Why not?!' he laughed.

As they walked side by side, they could hear the muffled sound of birds, and their boots crunched in rhythm through the snow and ice.

Dorothy asked about Si, Tess and Joe. Adam's step faltered, a shiver pulsed down his neck, his forehead furrowed momentarily. Although she could only see him through the corner of her eye, this didn't escape her notice.

'Ah pet, it's difficult, isn't it? You never mind me. Take no notice, it's none of my business.'

But he wanted to tell her that he and Si had found a quiet, dimly lit corner of the pub and after he'd hesitantly mentioned a childhood memory, one story had led to another and others, events, pranks, sorrows and heartbreaks until, inevitably, Adam mentioned the first time they had met Shubu.

'She was so cool, Si, bloody intelligent. I don't know why she fancied you mate!' They had laughed out loud.

Si had taken a moment to speak, breathing heavily, clearing his throat, palpably holding back tears, but then Adam found that Si couldn't stop talking about her.

Adam looked round at Dorothy and said, 'When Si broke down in tears, I thought I'd said too much. He was a mess. Next time I saw him, I was going to apologise but he launched straight into more memories about Shubu. He told me that either people ignore him or clam up whenever her name's mentioned, and he hates it.'

'Ah, pet. You've helped him a great deal. As I said before, sharing memories will help him to process it better. Stories are rather clever beings, aren't they?'

Adam nodded. They walked slowly, the watery ice slushing beneath their feet, as he continued, 'Tess is really struggling. Apparently, she and Si have shouting matches all the time, ending in floods of tears. Si says Joe doesn't say anything but listens to it all and is on high alert.'

Dorothy nodded. 'Tough for them all. By Tess's age stories can seem babyish can't they, and reading's been replaced with phones. They hold much more allure.' Dorothy was perceptive, without being judgmental. 'Hanging out with friends, focusing on appearance and how many likes they've got on social media is important.

'At this age, with brains expanding and hormones flying about, young people are sensitive to criticism and orders. We certainly have our work cut out for us to guide them without breaking down what can often feel like a fragile relationship between us.' Dorothy shook her head gently, as she opened and closed her fists and rubbed her hands together to stimulate the blood flow.

A flock of birds screeched overhead, black against the sky which had changed from pinks to a dull, endless grey.

Adam's feet were cold, so he stamped as they walked, to warm them.

'As Tess is 14, she's moving into the thinking

realms,' continued Dorothy. 'I'd suggest that mental and physical quizzes, quests and puzzles will help her. Anything that tests her knowledge and observation skills and challenges her thinking. Could you encourage her to go climbing and camping if she likes being outside?'

Adam nodded. He really wanted to support Si and was about to ask a question when Dorothy changed the subject.

'I thought that, since it's Tommy's seventh birthday in two weeks – what a special age – it's about time I shared my fifth secret with you. My first four secrets focused on what tools we can use to invent stories, while the next three concentrate on how we bring these tools to life.'

Adam wondered what this one could be.

'Yes, you're wondering!' Dorothy laughed. 'That's exactly what it is! This secret is about wonder and its importance, particularly in storytelling. Wonder is magical, delicious and... well, infectious too.'

Adam's mind flashed back to last week when Tommy had opened his curtains to see a world turned white! His first word had been 'Wow!' And that's exactly what Adam had felt too – a bubbling, infectious excitement about the snow.

'That's it!' Dorothy repeated, beaming. 'That's it! It's this quality of wonder that sparks our curiosity. Wonder is such a vital ingredient in effective learning, not only in literacy and numeracy, but for our whole development. It's a vital ingredient in the way we share stories with young children too. We want to build on their natural sense of wonder through our stories.'

Dorothy reminded Adam that when the storyteller uses words to paint the picture of a story, these images are readily transmitted to the listener. As we begin, '*Once upon a time...*' our listener, wide-eyed and open-mouthed, is transported to a far-away land.

'It's such a damp, grey morning,' Adam chuckled. 'I wish I could be carried away to an exotic land now!'

Dorothy readily agreed.

When Adam had first met Dorothy, he had stumbled and struggled to find words, been unable to think of ideas, but he realised that over the past few months he had practised and found it much easier to come up with stories, had built up a bigger bank of words. 'Mind you,' he said, 'the kids are quick to jump in with suggestions when I falter.'

'This is part of the fun of spontaneous storytelling isn't it, pet? The more we practise and enjoy the words the more easily they come to us. Good storytellers have a huge reservoir of vocabulary to bring stories alive and using these to tell a tale is part of the skill.' Dorothy urged Adam to find ways to evoke wonder in his storytelling. She explained that in doing so he would stimulate his kids' curiosity – a vital building block for them to become motivated and engaged adults. Dorothy rubbed the tip of her nose, which was icy cold, and continued.

'Then, as they inevitably go through more cynical stages of life, this inner light of wonder will continue to flicker. It will sustain them through their challenges and struggles.'

Adam thought about Tess and Joe. 'But what is wonder in stories? How do I do that? Is it the same as awe?' asked Adam, trying to reach for words to ask the right question.

'Good question,' said Dorothy. 'One to contemplate, for sure.'

Dorothy and Adam had a relaxed and playful way of being together, which had grown over time, allowing them to walk comfortably now in silence. The buildings on the side of the canal made way to open fields, exposing them to the bitter wind. Adam pulled his cap down as far as he could to stop the air biting at his ears.

Dorothy, oblivious to the cold, was considering Adam's question. 'Well, my sense is that awe is what we experience when we're in the presence of something vast or extraordinary. For example, witnessing a fiery sunrise or looking up at a million stars on a clear night. It's something outside of ourselves that we encounter. Whereas wonder is the feeling which lies inside us, often provoked by an awe-inspiring experience. For example holding your baby in your arms for the very first time. These two, awe and wonder, sit side by side.'

Dorothy could feel Adam's rising frustration as he wrestled with how to practically apply this information. 'OK, let's take two examples, how you prepare your environment and how you use your voice,' she continued as he sighed deeply, his irritation having been recognised by her. 'Create an environment which is calm, quiet, beautiful. If you have space in your home, choose a special nook as your story corner. Clear this space of clutter, except for one or two special treasures, like a candle which you gently light at the beginning of your story and blow out at the end. You could play a melodic instrument at the start and end of the story session, maybe collect flowers from the fields and arrange them in a tiny vase on a table or shelf which you drape with a silk cloth. Or place a few of the special stones, acorns or pinecones that the kids have collected next to the candle or vase.'

She drifted off for a moment, in her own thoughts, and then chuckled. 'Keep it natural and keep it simple. My wise grandmother used to say, "less is more". It's about keeping the space clean. Make sure there's no dust, put your attention into its beauty. Countless times I've seen the magic that this attention to detail brings, both to the teller and the listener.'

Adam thought about the Squidge Room. Perhaps Darinka and he could turn a corner of it into a story-telling space. He knew she would be up for it because she had become fascinated by stories and storytelling, learning and practising whenever possible.

'What about my voice? You mentioned using our voice?' asked Adam.

'Ah yes. What a good pupil you are this morning, Adam!' Dorothy joked.

'Well, you know Dinks, she'll be mad at me if I don't squeeze as much information from you as I can!' he bantered back. The two of them laughed out loud, sending birds scattering from a tree as they passed it. There was a dull roar of the traffic in the distance.

'Well, well, I better tell you then! How we use our voice is so important. You must be aware of the effect your voice has on the mood of your children. How they respond when your voice is angry, filled with joy or touched with sadness.'

Adam nodded.

'This is no different in storytelling. When you use a bright, bold, strong voice, you'll invoke energy, action and vitality,' said Dorothy. 'Dropping your voice and making it sinister will instil a touch of fear and dread. As Tommy gets older he'll enjoy more jeopardy in his stories!'

Dorothy stopped walking for a moment and touched Adam's arm.

'But don't overdo this with young ones, they don't need it, save it for another phase of their life, it will come soon enough.'

She started to walk again. 'When you use a quiet, gentle voice you'll lull the kids into a dreamlike state and draw out their sense of wonder.'

Adam thought about how different Darinka's story style was from his own. The kids seemed to like both.

'Since we associate wonder with pleasure, whatever we discover as a result of wonder is satisfying and energising.'

They walked on, watching and listening as the world around them awoke.

'Storytelling's a brilliant way for us to learn about the awe and wonder of the world. When we grow up, we might not remember the stories we were told when we were small, but we're likely to remember the sensory impression the story, and the teller, have left behind.'

Adam told Dorothy that he couldn't remember what stories, if any, his nan told him, but he could remember her smell and her warmth. When he was in trouble, as a lad, he would hide behind the sofa until she persuaded him to sit with her. Lost in her folds and her 'nan smell' she was silent as he wrestled with himself. Then she'd listen, without interrupting, as he spoke it all out. When he was around 13, he'd overheard her saying to his mum, 'He needs our love most when he deserves it least.' Adam scratched his chin as he swallowed away the lump in his throat and cracked two of his knuckles.

'Ah, pet, what a wise woman your nan was. She knew that children don't learn from what we say, but from what we do or feel and behind that, what we think. As she held you in her embrace, she was showing you that you were safe with her.' Dorothy made it sound so obvious!

'Holding hands does the same thing, pet.'

The wind was stirring, blowing strands of Dorothy's hair in all directions. She swept it out of her eyes and face, pinning it back up, as they walked.

'I could talk for hours about how important it is to cultivate wonder, to make time and space for these wow moments. To share joy with each other.' Dorothy's voice seemed to drop low and she spoke slowly and deliberately. 'Adam, really take notice of these moments in your life, the big and the small. When you consciously notice them, you're then able to incorporate this quality into your stories...' Dorothy paused, 'and your life... your life, Adam will be much happier.'

Dorothy laughed at herself as she rubbed her hands together.

'I have so much to say, don't I! But, creating these moments of wonder for your kids will make them feel more satisfied, more grateful and more inclined to help others.'

Adam knew that they were getting close to the warehouses. He slowed his pace, wanting to hear more.

Dorothy was still chatting. 'I know you want to hear something practical you can put into practice, don't you, young fella?'

Adam nodded and laughed. 'Yes! I do, to be fair!'

'So, here's a fun game to play with Tommy on his birthday. It's also a great rainy-day game. I call it "Finders-Keepers Treasure Hunt". It takes some preparation on your part but it's not difficult!'

'When Tommy comes down for breakfast on the morning of his birthday, place a small object, say a toy car, on the table. Attach a label with some words, like "Prepare for your Birthday Finders-Keepers Treasure Hunt". You could get the twins to draw round the words.'

'Then share a story with him to set up the game and send him off on his treasure hunt. The toy might lead him to the Squidge Room where all his toys are kept. In the Squidge Room there's another object-clue, with another little label. Perhaps a spoon? Tommy will need to think where the spoon comes from, and thus he opens the cutlery drawer to find the next object-clue. And in the drawer, there's another little note tied to, say, a bar of soap... and so to the bathroom...'

She stopped walking and looked directly at Adam. He paused too, taking in what she was describing.

'You get the idea, pet? It can have as many or as few clues as you like until eventually he gets a clue which brings him back to the breakfast table or somewhere hidden where he finds his birthday finders keepers present. Take care to put each clue somewhere safe so he doesn't inadvertently come across it ahead of time.'

'Or so the twins don't find them and tell him where they are!' added Adam, knowingly.

'Yes, indeed!'

As they started walking again Adam stamped his feet hard several times to keep them warm.

'But what kind of story would I tell?' asked Adam, whose brain had gone blank at the thought of this.

'Oh well, let's see. If it was Marija, it would definitely be a pirate story, wouldn't it?!'

Adam laughed. 'Oh yes, Marija's left our house and has been replaced by Demelza the Pirate.'

'Since Tommy was born in January you could use the time of year as a backdrop to the story. How about something like this...

'One bitter cold January morning when Squirrel Munch woke, he was very hungry so he visited his underground hoard to collect nuts, seeds and berries that he'd stored for the winter. To his surprise he couldn't find his hoard anywhere. He'd forgotten where he'd buried them. So he called for his friends, badger, rabbit and mouse to help.' Dorothy stopped for a moment. Adam could see she was making the story up as they walked. Both were aware how close they were to the warehouses. A noise of a plane cut through the story.

'They all agreed to help their friend,' continued Dorothy, 'but Squirrel Munch promised to share some of his food with whoever found it for him. "Finders keepers" said badger with a grin. They all set off to search. After a while Squirrel Munch was tired and headed back to his dray for a rest. Here he found an object with a note tied to it. It was a clue from rabbit.'

Adam now realised he could make something up, although he had secretly decided he would use this particular story for Tommy's birthday.

Dorothy concluded, 'This could be the toy that you've left out for Tommy, pet. So, you'd finish the story by saying that since Squirrel Munch didn't understand the clue, would Tommy help him by following the trail to find the buried treasure? Hopefully whatever story you create will entice him to start the hunt.'

'Tommy'll love this!'

'Perfect,' smiled Dorothy. 'Just perfect.'

They stopped again, this time outside the first of the three imposing warehouses where Adam would be working in the months ahead. Dorothy touched his shoulder gently. 'Adam, you're a good man, with a kind heart. Remember that.'

Adam's breath caught at the back of his throat. He stared ahead of him, afraid to look round at Dorothy in case he cried. For a split second he felt as if he was enveloped in his nan's arms.

Adam stayed motionless, unable to move, knowing that when he did eventually summon the courage to turn towards Dorothy, she would be gone.

Story Games from Chapter 5

Finders Keepers Treasure Hunt – see page 147
For one or more players (to be set up by someone who isn't playing)

- Gather several small objects from different rooms in your house and attach a label to each one.
- Decide on the order you will hide each object, where you intend to hide them and what the clues will be to enable players to move from one clue to the next.
- Write each clue on the appropriate label before hiding the objects to create a treasure hunt.
- Choose as many or as few clues as you like, the final clue leads to the prize.
- When the treasure hunt is prepared and the players are gathered, make up a story to set the scene, and to set up the game, sharing the first clue with them as part of the tale. They are now ready to set off on their treasure hunt.
- Each object prompts the players to the location of the next object. For example, if the first clue is a toothbrush, this encourages them to go to the bathroom to find the next clue and so on.

Did you know?
- Stop for a moment...
- As well as sharing stories, another way to reawaken our sense of awe and wonder is to be still, to do nothing except watch the world go by for a while. Many of us suffer from the pressures and stresses associated with modern life. Giving ourselves permission to integrate quiet time into our daily rhythm will help us

to unclutter our minds, dream, be creative and open ourselves to wonder afresh at our wonderful world. If you can find a place to sit, in nature, under a tree in the park, close to a stream or the canal or in the woods, even better!

Further reading...

The Artist's Way, by Julia Cameron.

Imagination, storytelling and the importance of wonder, by Ollie Oakenshield (watch on YouTube)

CHAPTER 6

Less is More
The Sixth Secret – Play

'Play is the highest form of research.'
Albert Einstein

Adam and Darinka had taken on board much of Dorothy's wise advice about rhythm and repetition, not only in stories but also in their daily life. By mid-June, as the days lengthened towards the summer solstice, they had settled into a healthy routine. Sometimes Darinka worried about what might be round the next corner, as everything seemed to be going a little too well.

She was really enjoying her new challenge – volunteering to work with individual pupils with additional speech and language needs, at New Park, the children's school. It gave her the opportunity to practise and adapt the story ideas, including the Story Bag, she'd learnt from Dorothy.

Although working on the warehouse conversion was intense and Adam was certainly putting in long hours, they were both pleased that the extra money was being saved towards their dream to buy a plot of land. Darinka and he agreed that he would leave early on Fridays to pick Tommy up from school.

Whilst Adam missed meeting the lads in the pub after work, he was surprised by how much fun he had with Tommy. The last three Fridays, he'd taken his son to the secluded lake nestled behind an old disused golf course at the other side of the village. Very few people knew about it, but Adam and Si had played there as kids. Tommy looked forward to being with his dad, on his own, playing water tag and volleyball. Adam was teaching Tommy to dive off the jetty.

Adam and Darinka had arranged to meet up after their swim for a family picnic, in the woods close to the lake. They had also done this for the past two weeks. The stream that ran through the woods was almost inaccessible due to a steep, bramble filled bank. However, in a few places the grassy banks rolled gently to the water's edge.

Darinka brought rugs and a large picnic feast which she and Adam laid out as the kids played together in the shallow water – paddling, building dams and creating a set of stepping stones. They shared stories, sang songs and told jokes. When Adam rigged up a tyre on a rope over one of the tree branches to use as a swing, Marija had not stopped talking about it all week.

Darinka had noticed the positive impact this time was having on Tommy, including him being kinder to his siblings and less anxious around adults. As the family came together in this special place, they eased gently into the weekend.

Before they'd met Dorothy, Darinka was always

thinking of new, exciting, and often expensive, things to keep the children occupied and stimulated. She would never have imagined doing such a simple activity, repetitively, would engage the children as much as it did.

They set up their camp under a large willow tree, which acted as a secret den. Here they were hidden away from the world, and if other families wandered into this area Adam became protective of the space.

'Adam, be nice.' Darinka would tug at his sleeve as he internally growled, or made crazy wild gestures, in an attempt to keep other families away, whilst also giggling at his foolishness.

Luka imitated his dad, calling out, much too loud, 'Go away, this is ours!' to Darinka's great embarrassment.

'Shut up,' Tommy had whispered to Luka who immediately lashed out at his brother, kicking him in the shin.

'Stop it now!' Adam said sternly to the boys. 'Stop it or we'll leave.'

Luka's habit of hitting and biting his brother and sister hadn't abated, despite Adam punishing him. Just a few days earlier Luka had punched Darinka in the leg.

She'd grabbed his hand and pulled him to one side. 'Luka, what are you doing? Don't hit, that's not nice, say sorry now.'

Luka had stuck his tongue out at her and broken free, running behind the sofa. Furiously Adam carried the crying boy, kicking and yelling, up to his bedroom. 'You stay there till you're ready to apologise. You don't do that to Mama, ever.'

As he was being carried away, Darinka wanted to

hug her son.

'You have to leave him there,' said Adam crossly. 'Otherwise, how's he ever going to learn it's not okay to hit and punch?'

Luka yelled out, thumping his bedroom door.

Darinka's heart was pounding. She was confused, anger towards Adam rising in her, even though she knew he was probably right. She wanted to speak with her mum or get advice from Dorothy.

The last time Adam had met Dorothy was almost four months ago along the canal. It was two months prior to that, at Mrs Oddie's Farm, when Darinka had last spoken with her.

Now, as they sat on the bank of the stream in the dappled sunlight, Luka was kicking again, despite having been contrite earlier in the week, promising never to do it again.

'Adam, there has to be a better way of dealing with Luka's outbursts. I don't understand what's happening to him, he's so angry. D'you think he's being bullied at school?'

'The teacher would have told us, wouldn't she? Let's just see if it changes. We just have to be clear, it's not acceptable. I used to hit out at his age too and I grew out of it.'

Darinka scoffed to herself, wondering if Adam really was so oblivious of his own outbursts. She decided to speak with Luka's teacher.

As they finished the remains of their picnic, Tommy and Luka continued to bicker. Tommy wouldn't drop it. 'You're a rude, naughty boy. You're not allowed any more cake.' As Tommy snatched the cake from

Luka's plate, Darinka cringed, recognising some of her own words and tone in Tommy's.

Adam stood up furiously. 'Enough! We're going home. I've had enough of you both.' Adam began to fold the rugs. 'Here Tommy, you carry that one.'

'It's not fair, why doesn't Luka have to carry anything?'

'He is going to carry one,' snapped Adam, handing Luka a rug, before striding off ahead of them all.

As Darinka and the children walked together, they were silent until Marija, holding her mum's hand, said, 'Luka'll feel better when we tell a story.' Darinka smiled softly and squeezed Marija's hand.

'Very wise words, *ljubica moja*, sweetheart.'

Adam calmed down quickly, slowing for the family to catch up with him.

'Sorry, Dada,' said Tommy, taking hold of his dad's hand.

'Yeah, me too. Sorry for getting angry,' Adam replied. He knelt down to Luka, looking the boy in the eyes. 'No more kicking matey, okay?'

'Okay, Dada,' Luka said, eyes on the ground.

They all walked together, hand in hand, and as they reached the hill close to home they spread out in a line, marching and singing their favourite hill song, *The Grand Old Duke of York*.

At their lime green door, Darinka reached out to touch Adam's hand. 'Will you take them to the stream next Friday, Adam? I'm off to London to meet Nataša and Vida... you remember?'

Darinka and her two school besties had been planning this trip for over a year. They'd booked into a small B&B close to Kings Cross for two nights. Nataša and Vida were flying in from Ljubljana, while Darinka would catch the bus to Leeds station, 15 miles away, and then take the train to London. She was excited, but also apprehensive because she hadn't stayed away from home without the children since Tommy was born.

Adam was also nervous, not sure how he would cope with the kids for a whole weekend, but he said, 'Of course I remember. It's no problem, stop worrying. I'll pick them all up and take them to the stream. We'll have a great time.' He paused and then added, sheepishly, conscious of how readily they had both slotted into the male/ female cliché, 'Will you make a picnic before you go? So, I can pick it up after work?'

'OK, since it's you,' she joked, having already thought about what she could prepare in advance to make it easier for Adam.

Friday was unusually hot and sticky, so Adam was pleased to be able to hang out near the stream, in the shade. They were lying on the rugs, their picnic spread around them, playing the cloud game when Dorothy joined them. Adam was always taken by surprise at her arrival, but the children took it in their stride.

'Hello Dotty, do you want some grapes?' Tommy had asked in a matter-of-fact way, handing the brown bag over to her, 'I'm going to finish my dam.' He made his way back down towards the stream.

'Thank you, kind sir, what a lovely idea.'

As she chatted to Adam, he told her how much more comfortable he was being on his own with his kids than he would have been a year ago. He put it down to them being older and easier to manage.

'And you, finding your place as their father,' Dorothy added in recognition of his determination to improve as a parent.

Adam's face flushed and then he snorted, as if pushing her comment away.

'Can we play one of your story games Dotty?' Marija asked.

Dorothy smiled and winked. 'Marija, I have the perfect game for us to play. It's called the Disrupter, come and help me.'

Luka rushed towards Dorothy, pushing Marija out of the way, almost knocking her over.

Marija yelled out. Dorothy held open her arms for the little girl and before Adam had a chance to scold Luka, she signalled to the little boy to join her too.

'Oh dear, are you okay,' she said to both children simultaneously, stroking Luka's arm gently.

Immediately, and without prompting, Luka leant over to stroke his sister's arm, as if by way of apology. Marija gave Luka a kiss.

Dorothy continued as if nothing unusual had happened. 'So, I'll start a story. You think of a word to call out to me and I'll add it in to the story. Once I've put that word in, give me another word. Can you do that?'

'Yes,' Marija said confidently, as Luka nodded. They were sitting next to her, their hands full of grapes.

'Come, Tommy, story time,' Marija called out, but Tommy was busy manoeuvring a large log across the water to create his dam.

Dorothy began. 'Once upon a time there was a little cottage on the edge of the woods. Out of the chimney came the curling smoke from the fire.' Dorothy hadn't said any more when Tommy called over.

'Dustbin lid.'

Adam laughed – Tommy didn't miss a trick.

'This little cottage was owned by Arty, a pixie. Arty was a very special pixie whose job it was to collect up the rubbish left in the woods and to put it in a big dustbin ready for collection. Arty made sure there wasn't any mess left after each weekend. One day –'

'Pillow,' called out Adam.

'One day, they were putting the rubbish in the dustbin when they realised that the dustbin lid was missing.' The children giggled.

'Sausanges,' said Luka happily, mispronouncing the word. Dorothy smiled and continued.

'"Well," said Arty, "I'm going to have to cover up the rubbish, so the foxes don't take it all out. I know – I'll use my pillow." Whilst Arty was making it secure, he wondered what he'd have for tea...'

'Sausanges,' Marija repeated.

'Of course – "Oh yes," said Arty, "that's exactly what I'll cook for my tea."' Dorothy smiled as the children threw more and more words at her, which she wove into the tale.

Adam was as involved in the story as the children, so when Dorothy asked him to take over the story, he instantly took the challenge.

'This is a great game, Dada,' said Tommy, who had left his dam to join in. 'I'm going to tell Mrs Farmery. She likes my story games.'

Mrs Farmery, Tommy's teacher, had mentioned to Darinka how engaged Tommy was at story time. His ability to concentrate and his writing skills had improved dramatically in the past few weeks.

Dorothy continued to play the Disrupter game, until the children took themselves off to play in the water. As they chatted happily to each other, Marija and Luka held hands, something they hadn't done for a while.

Adam had been waiting to ask Dorothy about Luka hitting out and how she'd diffused the situation so effortlessly.

'It's a strange thing pet, but sometimes when little children lash out it hasn't got anything to do with the current situation. When we ask them why, they can't answer that question; their brain doesn't yet have the capacity for this kind of reasoning. They can imitate and tell us what they believe we want to hear, but it's unlikely to be the real reason.'

Adam listened, doubtful.

'In my experience,' continued Dorothy, 'children are exposed to all kinds of violence and aggression, in all kinds of ways, throughout each and every day. For example, us shouting at them, or around them. Even raising our voices. Can you imagine how very large we are in comparison to a one-and two-year-old? We must seem like giants. So, a raised arm or voice has an impact. They see and hear loud noises all the time, even when it's not directed at them – on TV, in the playground, between siblings, with a dog who's barking aggressively at the garden gate...'

As if on cue there was a thunderous, rumbling sound of a plane overhead. Dorothy and Adam chuckled. He cracked his knuckles, which he often did when he was nervous or concentrating. Dorothy continued.

'Small children take this, and every other kind of emotion and feeling, into their bodies. As they remember and reconnect to a violent action they might have the impulse to lash out, perhaps by hitting or biting, in an attempt to get it out of their bodies.'

Adam pulled at the grass as he thought about all the times Darinka and he shouted, even if it was only from downstairs to upstairs, not to mention his outbursts and quick temper. His face flushed at the thought.

Dorothy smiled, pausing in case Adam wanted to speak, but when he remained silent, looking down at the ground, she went on.

'Now we can't protect them against all these things, but what we can do is be mindful of how we respond if they do hit out. If we grab them or use aggressive, jerky actions, shout and get angry with them, all we're doing is multiplying and magnifying that same feeling within them. However, if we can find compassion for them and speak gently and kindly, this will help them change their responses to situations.'

'I saw you stroke Luka when he pushed Marija,' said Adam.

'Yes pet, so first I check that Marija is okay and safe, but then I want to make sure that Luka is okay too. He has suffered as much as the person he's pushed. Do you see that?'

Adam wasn't sure, but he had just witnessed how Dorothy's way of dealing with the situation had been more successful than his own methods, causing Luka to be kind to his sister without being asked. He wanted to try this method, although he knew it would take a great deal of effort on his part.

'Do. Do try it for yourself – the more you practise the easier it will become,' Dorothy suggested. 'By being gentle with him when he makes these mistakes you will put in the gesture of kindness and help him to release whatever his angry impulse might have been.'

Adam thought about his nan's words. 'He needs our love most when he deserves it least.' Adam looked across at the children as he heard them laughing, making up a story, clearly influenced by the storytelling earlier.

'I get it with little kids, but what about when Tommy is a pain or just plain naughty? Surely, he should know better by now. That makes me cross.'

Dorothy was silent for a moment, as if considering the question. 'This is an interesting question. So, firstly, he is still little, he's only seven years old. We expect a great deal from our first born. It's also important to remember that when you're dealing with what you might call rudeness or naughtiness, it's not Tommy who is *naughty*. He might have done something you don't like but that's his action rather than him being a naughty boy. It's vital to separate the boy from the action. One way you could deal with it is to imagine that he has a naughty imp on his shoulder. In this way you can ask him to blow away the *naughty, angry or cheeky imp* so he can easily return to a place of balance.'

Dorothy brushed her own shoulder as if flicking dust off it as Adam watched her closely.

'A really powerful way of helping children with

challenging behaviour,' she continued, 'is to create a story, perhaps about the naughty imp, which addresses that particular behaviour, not in an overt or preachy way – that never works – but in a subtle way.'

Adam lay back on the rug, wondering if he would remember this in the heat of the moment. He closed his eyes as the warmth of the sun, filtering through the leaves of the willow, fell on his face. There was a stillness to the day, which made everything seem possible.

The two of them sat together for what seemed like a long time. The birds chirped and chatted and squabbled in the trees around them. Dorothy watched the children play.

'What are you planning this weekend?' Dorothy asked, breaking the silence, as she pulled her knitting from her big patchwork bag. The birds scattered in all directions at this sudden movement.

Adam said he hadn't thought about what to do. 'I'm not very good at keeping them amused. I might take them to the cinema. I've had such a busy week, I don't feel like doing anything, but that's not an option with kids is it?'

'Ah, true, true.' She said as her needles began their steady, soothing click.

'I think there are lots of people who feel this way. We live in a world where we believe it's necessary to fill our children's days with activities and adventures, don't we? But it's important for them to slow down their nervous systems and rest. Tension is never good for learning.'

'When I was a kid, my mum didn't take me to places,' said Adam. 'Si and I played out most of the time, so I don't really know what to do with them. Darinka usually organises it.'

Dorothy smiled. 'Well, maybe this weekend you could do something radical?'

Adam sat up, leaning back on his elbows. 'I'm up for that!' he declared, a mischievous grin sweeping across his face.

Dorothy shared with Adam an experiment that had taken place, almost two decades earlier, in a German kindergarten. A nursery school that had made the decision to remove all the toys from the classroom for three months.*

Adam sat upright.

'The reason they did this experiment was to see if this would be better for the children's creativity, problem-solving abilities and social skills,' she explained.

Adam immediately thought about their Squidge Room, full of toys. He'd hoped the kids would use the room to play in but, in fact, since they cleared it out it had barely been used. 'Did it work, this experiment?' he asked.

'Well, pet, apparently it did. Although it took time for the children to adapt, of course, but soon they were using the chairs and blankets to create dens.

'By the end of the experiment the children were completely involved in their imaginative play. The research showed they were able to concentrate better and communicate more effectively.' Dorothy looked

---

* The project was called *Der Spielzeugfreie Kindergarten* (the nursery without toys) founded by Rainer Strick and Elke Schubert.

down at her knitting, picking up a dropped stitch. 'What most of us forget, pet, is that play is in the child, not in the toy.'

'So, are you suggesting that I get rid of all the children's toys over the weekend? To be fair that is pretty radical.' He laughed nervously, thinking back to an incident that had happened earlier in the year. 'I've tried it already! Didn't go down too well...'

Dorothy's eyes danced, encouraging Adam to continue.

'I came home from work one day to find the kids fighting over some toy or other. Dinks was tired and frustrated and I wanted to help, so dived straight in. I told them that if they didn't stop, I'd throw all their toys away. I grabbed the one they were fighting over and put it in the bin.'

He went on to explain that he had ordered all three children to choose five toys each and, even when Darinka had shouted at him to stop, he'd found it impossible to back down.

Dorothy rested her knitting on her lap as she listened.

Adam sighed heavily, more serious now. 'Not my finest hour, as you can imagine. The children went to bed sobbing. Dinks and I rowed all evening and she threatened that if I didn't sort out my temper, she'd take the children back to Slovenia. She was so cross it took days before we were speaking to one another properly. It was horrific to be honest!'

When he'd finished speaking Dorothy brought her tin of mints out of her pocket and offered one to him, taking one for herself. 'Well pet! I wasn't thinking of being that radical! I thought more along the lines of leaving them to play freely, uninterrupted, for a day.' They both laughed, lightening his mood.

'I can see why you'd like to remove many of their toys,' she continued, 'but as you discovered, taking them away as part of a punishment isn't the best way to begin, is it, pet? Threats and punishments are short term fixes, which only build up resentment for later down the line.'

Adam felt foolish and ashamed, but because Dorothy smiled gently, listening without judgement, he was more able to laugh at himself and admit his failings.

'I don't know how I would ever begin to raise it again with Dinks, she'd go ballistic.' He looked over at the children, still totally absorbed in their game, and back towards Dorothy. Looking at her sheepishly, he asked, 'What would you do?'

Dorothy thought for a moment. 'Mmm, pet, that's a difficult one. Having fewer toys or deciding to reduce the number of activities children are involved in, needs to be a conscious choice. We live in a *more is better* society don't we? It would have to be something that you both consider and implement carefully. I know you like things to be open and shut, pet, but here I don't have any easy answers, I'm afraid.' She shook her head gently.

It was true Adam did like things to be straightforward and clear-cut so he was disappointed that Dorothy hadn't given him a concrete answer.

'The thing is, pet,' she continued, 'the golden age of play is between the ages of three and six years old. Playing is a natural part of a child's development, which keeps them active, well and happy. What's more, children need unstructured play opportunities from birth until they're teenagers.'

When Adam was with Dorothy, it was as if time stood still.

'When children are left to play freely and without instruction or guidance, they learn many life skills,' she said. 'What I know is that when children have a large number of toys these become a distraction. When children are distracted, they don't learn or play well. As I said, the play is in the child not in the toy.'

Marija's piercing scream shattered the quiet. Tommy was tugging on her t-shirt while Luka was hitting Tommy.

Adam jumped up instantly. 'What are you doing?' he called out, 'Tommy stop that now!'

The children ran up the bank, shouting and blaming each other. Dorothy, who'd also stood, leant out to touch Adam's arm. He swung round to look at her soft, gentle face, took a sharp intake of breath and paused.

Dorothy looked earnestly at the three children and said, 'I bet you're able to work this out for yourselves, aren't you? It seems to me you're very smart.'

Tommy came over and said, in a grown-up sort of way, 'It's worse when adults get involved... they don't know what they're doing really.' With that he turned round, calling to Marija and Luka to join him. 'Come on, we've got work to do, it isn't easy you know.' The twins obediently followed their brother back to the stream where he proceeded to give instructions.

Dorothy winked at Adam, chuckling to herself. She sat back down and smoothed out her skirt and, feeling a slight chill, she wrapped her shawl round her knees.

Adam's mouth had dropped open. 'What just happened there?'

'Well. Well, in my experience, when we adults try to protect children and sort out their disputes, we deprive them of the opportunity to learn how to take care of themselves and resolve their own quarrels. Sometimes of course we have to step in, but many times we make it much worse, particularly if we make assumptions and don't know all the facts. Tommy's already worked that out for himself hasn't he? What a smart lad he is.' Dorothy picked up her knitting again.

'This is why I can't stress enough how important play is for children,' she said.

'So, is play one of your seven secrets?' Adam asked bluntly.

'Yes. Oh, yes, it is,' answered Dorothy enthusiastically. 'It's my sixth secret. Play is an intrinsic part of storytelling and is crucial for children. Not only do they practice social and emotional skills, including how to manage their emotions, but while they're creating their stories, they can come up with new ideas and inventions.'

Dorothy continued. 'We want our children to question and be curious so they can work out how they fit into the world and what their role is. The child who has the opportunity to play, and to invent stories, is likely to become an adult full of focus and drive. See them now, they're lost in their own universe!'

She giggled as she watched them and wiped away a wisp of hair from her face as Adam grabbed his hoody.

The heat had gone out of the sun and he was suddenly chilly in the shade. He called to the children to come and put their jumpers on too, but they ignored him.

Dorothy began to roll up her knitting to put away in her bag. Adam was about to call the kids again when Tommy called out.

'Dada, help me with this log. We can't move it.'

Adam jumped up.

'Okay, let's see what we can do, but when we've done this it's time to go home. Okay?'

'I helping,' said Marija feistily.

'Yes, we definitely need your help,' Adam told her as he showed them what to do.

'It's physics,' he said earnestly to the children. 'If you use this as a fulcrum you can lift it more easily. Watch Tommy. You watch too, Marija.'

Luka had wandered over to Dorothy, searching for some popcorn. 'This is a dinosaur.' he held a piece up and then put it in Dotty's mouth.

'This one is a snail,' she reciprocated, popping it into Luka's mouth. He giggled, continuing the game.

When the log was in place, Adam stood in the stream, which was not as full as it had been a few weeks ago because of the recent dry weather. He put his hands on his hips, surveying his work. Tommy and Marija did likewise.

'Good work, gang!' he said, as he climbed back up the grassy bank.

'Darinka's going to be cross she missed you,' he said to Dorothy as he started gathering up the food remains into the basket.

'I bet she's having a marvellous time with her pals,' said Dorothy, standing up and rolling her shoulders, stiff from sitting.

'Remember,' she said, helping him to gather their belongings, 'that when a child is exploring, they are seeking to discover, *What does this toy do?* Once they've worked this out, they next want to discover, *What can I do with this toy?*'

'Ah, it makes sense then,' Adam said, collecting the rubbish up into one bag, 'that when children are surrounded by too many toys, they spend more time exploring and less time playing.' Adam was frustrated that Darinka wasn't with them, certain she'd agree to his cull if she had been. He felt somewhat vindicated that his instinct was right but cross with himself for his clumsy and failed execution.

Dorothy sighed and nodded, as the children ran up to join them. Luka threw himself against her, wanting a cuddle and Marija, shivering, wet from top to toe, stretched out her arms towards her dad.

'We did it, Dada, Demelza did it.'

He knelt down and drew his daughter towards him, scooping her up. Darinka had packed fluffy towelling robes for each of the kids but had told Adam that Marija would probably be the only one who would need it.

As he helped her into her red, hooded poncho, wrapping his warm arms around her, he replied, 'Demelza and you have done brilliant work, Pirate Marija.'

'I'm not Marija, I'm Demelza,' she corrected him. He laughed and kissed her, 'Oh of course, silly me!' He stood up, gesturing to the boys.

'Let's get this stuff together, gang,' he said, handing over a towel or bag for each of the children to carry. After his conversation with Dorothy, he was really looking forward to the weekend ahead.

He turned to her, his eyes smiling brightly. 'So you're saying that by providing fewer toys, we give them more time to play?' Then he giggled and said, 'It's going to be tough to stop myself from throwing everything out whilst the children are sleeping and Dinks is away!'

Dorothy chuckled too. 'Mmm, I think, perhaps, you know that's not the best way forwards. But I tell you what. Why don't you start by spending a whole day at home, without computers, television or the like? Maybe you could find inventive ways to create music together, with a comb and tissue paper, a dustbin lid and stick, a bottle with peas inside? Or you could introduce them to tongue twisters, and riddles. I bet Tommy would love that, he's at the perfect age. But don't give him the answer straight away. Let him wrestle with it, maybe until the following day – it's great brain gym!'

Tommy was listening, and joined in, 'Oh yes, let's make some drums, Dada! And I've got a riddle for you!'

Adam imagined his neighbours never speaking to him again if they played drums for a whole day. He told Tommy that he wanted to hear the riddle on their way home.

Dorothy was amused by his facial expression and continued. 'When you've had breakfast, walked, played together for a while, then get on with your own work, making or mending something, ideally in the same room as them. You'll be surprised how quickly they'll start to do their own work too.'

'Bye Dotty,' Tommy said, standing next to his dad, smiling.

'Goodbye, pet. I hope you have the most magical weekend.' She picked up her bag and as she turned to walk along the stream she said, 'One more tip, Adam, if you can bear it!'

He laughed.

'If you're on the computer or telephone, it won't work. You have to be emotionally available to them,' she said, and winked.

Adam and the children stood together, waving good-bye. 'Bye Dotty!'

When she'd turned the bend, Adam picked up the basket and bags. 'Come on you lot, let's get cracking. It's nearly time for bed.'

They walked slowly in the opposite direction from Dotty. Luka tugged at his dad's sleeve and said cheekily, 'No, it's not, it time for a story.'

Adam laughed out loud. 'You're right, mate, and then a riddle.' He nodded towards Tommy. 'What's that game called again... The Disrupter? Okay... I'll start...'

Tommy immediately shouted out, 'Engine.'

'Hang on, hang on!' Adam laughed. 'I haven't started the story yet!'

STORY GAMES FROM CHAPTER 6

The Disrupter – see page 159

For two or more players

- The first player begins to share a spontaneous story.
- The listeners call out random words, which the first player incorporates into their story. The listeners call out one random word at a time. Once this has been included in the story, listeners can add another disrupting word.
- Depending how many people are playing, give listeners the chance to become the teller, including the option of having two tellers sharing a story.

Tongue Twisters– see page 172

For one or more players

There are many wonderful tongue twisters, both long and short. Here are a few to begin.

- Start by saying the phrase slowly, repeatedly, speeding up as you get more proficient.
- You could try adding two together and alternating between them. You might find that some are easier than others.

Whether the weather be fine
or whether the weather be not.
Whether the weather be cold
or whether the weather be hot.
We'll weather the weather
Whatever the weather
whether we like it or not.

Sly Sam sips Sally's soup

Mixed Biscuits

Red Lorry Yellow Lorry

Riddles– see page 172
For two or more players
I really recommend sharing riddles with children, aged seven plus. Riddles are fun but they're more beneficial than you might at first think.

Riddles can support children's problem solving, logic and critical thinking skills. If we wrestle with a riddle for a period of time it can help our concentration, focus and brain dexterity. They have also been shown to improve children's comprehension and creativity as they hear new words and new ways to use them, subliminally learning rhythm and rhyming.

I suggest that you don't give the answer away too quickly, otherwise many of the benefits are lost...

• *What starts with 'P', ends with 'E' and has a million letters in it?*

Did you know?
Why play is so important for children:
• 'Play is at the core of the development of the child,' explains Syeda Sazia Zaman and Ferdousi Khanom, education and child development experts. Children experience and learn about their world through play: they explore their physical environment, express their emotions and build their vocabulary through playful

moments. 'Play is very natural for children around the world,' adds Khanom. 'It is a really important tool for children's cognitive, physical, social and emotional development and also their imagination and creativity.'

Further reading...

Healing Stories for Challenging Behaviour, by Susan Perrow.

Impro for Storytellers, by Keith Johnson.

Theater Games for the Classroom: A teacher's handbook, by Viola Spolin.

'What is free play and why should you encourage it at home?' by Syeda Sazia Zaman and Ferdousi Khanom.

CHAPTER 7

One Step at a Time
The Seventh Secret – Confidence

'We know what we are but know not what we may be.'
William Shakespeare

Darinka was sitting on a bench on the village green, across from the school gates, eating her lunch, when she felt Dorothy's presence next to her. She rolled her eyes, shook her head in disbelief and chuckled at Dorothy's magical appearance.

'It's almost a year since I first met you,' Darinka said, beaming. 'I was disappointed not to see you down by the stream. I think Adam was disappointed that we weren't all together too. He couldn't wait to tell me what you'd said about the toys. We ended up deciding to store several of them in the attic and to stop buying so many. Of course, it won't surprise you to hear that the kids haven't missed them! They're playing even more in the Squidge Room since I upturned the table and left a pile of cloths, rugs and pillows next to it.'

'Oh, I can imagine. What a treat to build a den.

Is it really a year, pet? My, my, what a year it's been, eh?' said Dorothy.

Darinka nodded. Her life had changed considerably since their first encounter at the windmill last summer. Tommy was enjoying being in Year Two and the twins would be in school full time from September. Adam was working hard on the warehouse project and had recently had confirmation that after the first development was complete, he would be working on the second one. Darinka had recently started working alongside the Year Three teacher, Miss Winker, as her teaching assistant when the job unexpectedly became available. Although she had been very apprehensive in the first few weeks, having not worked while her kids were young, she was invigorated by the challenge. Now, as the summer holidays were approaching, she knew she would miss the camaraderie and community.

Dorothy listened as Darinka chatted on, eager to share her experiences.

'Oh, I was shaking so much the first time Miss Winker asked me to tell a story in class,' Darinka said.

When Miss Winker had realised that Darinka was a natural storyteller, she had asked her to play the ABC story game Darinka had demonstrated in her interview.

'Now she wants me to introduce more story games, including my Story Bag. But can you suggest a good one for around fifteen children?'

They could suddenly hear a cacophony of children's voices as they came out into the playground from lunch. It distracted them both for a while until Dorothy said, 'How about *The Story Pot*? This story game can be played with any number of people. Mind you, it's a long time since I played it!'

Dorothy described the game as Darinka ate the last of her sandwich. 'First you divide the children into groups, maybe groups of three. Give them a piece of paper and a pencil. Each team decides upon a name, an animal, an object and a place between them, as follows:

'Firstly, you ask them to write down a name beginning with a letter of the alphabet that you decide. For example, G.

'Each team tells you which name they've chosen. If more than one team picks the same name it isn't added to the story pot. However, any suggestion which is unique to one team goes into the story pot. Next ask them to choose an animal, beginning with another letter of the alphabet. For example, D. They choose an animal, team by team. Again, only put the animals in that haven't been picked by more than one team.' Dorothy paused for a moment, smiling. 'Does this make any sense?'

Darinka nodded. 'Yes I think so.' She licked her fingers, one by one, as she finished her sandwich.

'Good. Well then, continue with the objects and places, using the same method. Find containers – I use teapots – to put the words into. The stories can now begin. Ask different children to draw out a word from each of the containers, one by one, to stimulate a story.

'Oh, I love the sound of this,' said Darinka. 'That's brilliant, thank you!'

Dorothy laughed. 'You're welcome, pet. I often add a number of connective words to the pot too. For example, meanwhile, but, however, later, besides... These words really help the children move the story forwards. See how you get on.'

'Do I need to explain all the rules to them before we begin?'

'I tend not to give too many instructions in advance, as it can be more confusing for young children,' explained Dorothy. 'Mind you, in Year Three they are beginning to want more rules. Start with the first part and take it step by step, building up the game as you go. They'll soon pick it up, if you're confident about it. Of course, the more you play the better the game will become and the more language the children will learn and use.'

'I'll try it this afternoon.' Darinka stood up to brush the crumbs from her skirt and put the paper bag in the bin next to the bench, still speaking. 'It was great because after I played the ABC game a few times Miss Winker noticed an improvement in the children's vocabulary. It gave me a real confidence boost. I want to share more stories and story games with them.'

'Well, that's excellent,' Dorothy said with such vigour that Darinka laughed. 'There are endless ways you can interchange these story games.'

Darinka glanced down at her watch; it was almost the end of her lunch break. She pulled a satsuma from her bag. As she started to peel it, Dorothy commented on the fresh burst of citrus. Darinka offered her half but Dorothy shook her head, smiling.

'No thanks, I've just finished a mint,' she said.

Dorothy held her hand to her chest, as if she was overcome with emotion. 'We've come to my final secret, pet. It's the secret of confidence, but it seems to me that you're already working on this.'

Darinka lowered her eyes, pleased to receive

praise but embarrassed to openly acknowledge her progress and disappointed to hear that she might not see Dorothy again.

The Wise Woman continued. 'I always think that this secret should be both the first and the last. We need to have the confidence to give storytelling a go, but it's only when we start to tell stories that we realise all we need is confidence!'

Darinka nodded, understanding this now.

'When I think back to all the times I've shared these secrets, pet, the most common barrier to making up stories is almost always a lack of confidence. People often tell me that they're happy to create stories for children but freeze when other adults are watching.'

Darinka nodded again and smiled broadly, having experienced this for herself. It was one thing to make up tales with her own children, but quite another now, in school, sharing a story in front of the other teachers, which she found terrifying.

'I haven't told you yet,' she said, 'but last week Mrs Cowl, our head teacher, asked me to share a story in assembly at the last minute.' Darinka said that because she hadn't got any time to prepare, she'd decided to do a spontaneous story, using one of Tommy's finger puppets, which she admitted to having appropriated!

'It's about judgement isn't it, pet?' said Dorothy. 'We don't feel judged by young children because they're living in this realm of make-believe themselves. But with adults, if our inner critic takes hold, we censor ourselves and lose confidence. It's at this point that we decide our stories aren't good enough and imagine those listening are judging us. This is the best way to block any creativity.' Dorothy had a way of making Darinka feel more empowered. 'My wise grandmother used to say that "In the forest a mighty oak never compares itself to a slender willow, so why do we compare ourselves to others?" I agree with her, it's such a waste of our precious energy. We all have our own unique voice, pet. You're finding yours. Trust yourself.'

Darinka felt the prickling of the satsuma on her lips as a tingle ran down her spine.

'So how did it go, your story?'

'I was a bit disappointed with myself as it wasn't very good. Although now you talk about an inner critic, mine was in full swing that day,' she giggled and continued, 'but, I did remember to use my senses and my memories, which helped a lot, and one of the finger puppets, which I love. Tommy told me afterwards that his classmates had agreed that he had the coolest mum.'

Dorothy lent over and touched Darinka's arm, as if to make sure that she understood what a compliment this was. Darinka also remembered that Rachel had phoned, later in the evening, to say that Lucy had talked about it all the way home. Darinka breathed heavily.

'I was so relieved and so... so... grateful to you, Dorothy. Thank you, you've helped me more than you know.'

'You should be very proud of yourself, pet. You're the one that has taken my suggestions and turned them into reality. You're the one with the courage.'

Dorothy took hold of Darinka's hands, holding them in her own for a moment.

'You are a very special young woman, the children are lucky to have you with them.'

Darinka's eyes swelled with tears and one trickled

down her cheek. She couldn't speak because she knew she wouldn't be able to stop them.

Dorothy's voice was upbeat now and full of energy. 'I know what will help you. Instead of worrying about whether or not you can come up with a good story, drop all the chatter in your head by breathing into your heart. Relax and listen. Imagine that the tale is coming to you and through you, rather than from you. This will make a big difference to your confidence.'

Darinka turned and looked directly into Dorothy's deep eyes. 'I think what you're saying is that by taking my ego out of the story, it's easier to let the images and words come to me?'

Dorothy smiled back, her eyes dancing, soft and kind, and nodded. 'As my Wise Grandmother used to say, "it's not about you, it's about the story".'

Dorothy and Darinka laughed loudly and for quite some time.

The time was ticking up towards one o'clock. Darinka had so much she wanted to ask and share with Dorothy before she had to head back into school.

'Stories are powerful, aren't they, pet?' Dorothy said. 'You can do so much good for children and adults by sharing stories with them. And the wonderful thing is, the more confidence you have in yourself the more stories you'll share and the better storyteller you'll become. It's a wonderful circle!'

Darinka asked what to do if a child called out, interrupting the story, wanting to know what a particular word meant.

Dorothy said she'd rather explain the word as part of the story instead of stopping to explain. 'What

I find, is that if you share the story with confidence, children will listen, hear and make sense of words even if they don't know exactly what they mean. It's to do with context, tone and delivery. If you introduce words that are new then you can repeat those words and use another word, meaning the same thing, immediately afterwards. You could also use a gesture to help them understand the word.'

Darinka had watched as Miss Winker told a story, the children sitting in silence, waiting for the next word, drinking it up.

'It's wonderful that you're asking questions, Darinka,' said Dorothy. 'Wonderful that you're so curious. It's our curiosity which opens our imagination. I sense that you're really open to share your gift with these children aren't you?'

Darinka cast her mind back to last summer, when she had struggled to think of anything to share with her own three, let alone with a whole class full of children. 'I felt useless. I remember what you said to me. You said, "We all have different strengths and weaknesses. Focus on the skills you have, rather than those you think are missing."' She sighed heavily. 'You encouraged me to tell stories in Slovene or German. So many people, including my own family, said the same. I'm not sure now why I didn't, but it was another thing I would use to beat myself up.' Darinka swallowed hard and shuffled, pulling pieces of her satsuma peel into smaller pieces. The zesty smell that was released calmed her a little. Dorothy remained silent, so Darinka continued.

'I sang one or two of my favourite lullabies to

Tommy when he was tiny, but I worried that he'd get confused between the two languages. I thought about it again after you'd spoken with Adam and decided to give it a go in school. I asked Miss Winker's permission to include a German rhyme in my story.'

'And?' Dorothy asked when Darinka paused.

'To be honest, the children were bewildered. They didn't get it, so, although I know you told me to use gestures and repeat the verse twice – I lost my nerve. I haven't done it since.'

Dorothy was quiet for a while, looking across the green at the other teachers, some chatting and laughing in groups as they headed back towards the school gates. One of the teaching assistants looked across at Darinka and waved.

'It's easy to give up when it appears not to have worked first time, isn't it, pet? But remember what I said before – when we teach our children to clean their teeth, we don't just ask them once and then, if they won't do it, we give up.' They both laughed. 'Well, it's the same when we introduce any new idea or new practice. Language acquisition takes time and patience and... repetition, repetition, repetition! Don't give up. Remember the rule of three. Bear in mind that when you're unsure, the children will feel less safe.'

Darinka wondered if she would have the confidence to try again.

'One step at a time, eh? Try this...' Dorothy urged. 'Share a short, seasonal rhyme in English, repeat it a couple of times and then do the same rhyme in German, always using the same gestures, so the children know it's the same rhyme.'

Darinka stood up and threw her peel into the bin, anxious that she needed to go back to school. She spoke so quickly she was falling over her words.

'Oh, I should tell you, I've booked flights to Slovenia. I'm taking the children to visit my mum. We're going to stay for three weeks, and I think Adam will come over for a while. I can't wait. It's been so long since I've visited for more than a weekend. The twins have never been on a plane. They won't remember their *Babica*... Mum cried when I told her.'

'Oh, now that is exciting, pet. So, it's the perfect time to share stories and songs with your three, in Slovene.'

'I was going to wait till we're over there and then maybe it will be more natural?' Darinka asked, almost as a question.

Dorothy stood up too, gathering her shawl around her shoulders. The clouds had all but gone and the sky was deep blue. 'Follow your instincts, but check first that it isn't about lack of confidence. If you're unsure, they'll immediately pick up on that. But, if you believe that sharing your mother tongue is in your children's best interests then, although there might be initial resistance, I'd recommend you persevere. Being clear what your intention is for the story – for bedtime, a transition, or to soothe a fear – will make it easier to choose the right story. You'll be surprised how easily they'll follow the meaning from your intention, your tone and your gestures.'

Darinka always came away from her conversations with Dorothy inspired, but with so much to process and digest.

'When a child learns something new, like a

language or musical instrument,' Dorothy explained, 'it requires their full attention. This then fires their imagination. You know what it's like when you conquer a new challenge – you feel more confident in your abilities. Well, of course this is the same for children, pet.' Dorothy had so little time left to share her knowledge.

The two women began to walk slowly towards the school gate. Dorothy continued. 'My Wise Grandmother used to say that our stories, and the stories we tell ourselves, form a powerful sense of who we are and who we will become. Stories can inspire the very best in children, enabling them to be more than they thought possible. My wish is that through our words, our creativity and our love, we can give them the confidence to be themselves, because confidence is vital to health and wellbeing.'

Darinka wished she'd had a teacher or grandparent like Dorothy. When she was growing up, she constantly doubted herself. She was still unsure when she had first arrived in the UK and felt very alone with only Adam to lean on. Now things were changing and she definitely believed in herself more. 'I still have a touch of imposter syndrome!' She laughed. They were close to the gates.

'I better get back into school – I've got stories to tell!'

The two women hugged one another.

Just before I go,' said Darinka, 'can I ask you one more question? If you had to think of one thing to help me increase my confidence in telling stories, what would it be?'

'Oh, well now, that is a good question,' Dorothy

chuckled, squeezing her eyes tight shut, concentrating, thinking of what this might be. 'So, off the top of my head, I would say, remember that we're all storytellers. Sharing stories is an important part of what makes us human. Our brains work to build stories, whether those are pictures, words or numbers – we make connections from one idea to the next.'

Darinka looked puzzled.

'Well, pet, if I started to share an interesting anecdote about myself and stopped halfway through the story, you'd find that, not only is it frustrating, but the chances are your brain would try to resolve or finish the story for you.'

'Oh, yes I can see that,' said Darinka, sipping water from her bottle and trying not to look at her watch again, knowing that Dorothy would never be hurried.

'Stories are all around us – in nature, in business, in advertising, when we meet in the pub, or collect our children from school,' Dorothy chuckled as she concluded. 'Let's face it, pet, politicians the world over tell tales all the time!'

The women giggled, Darinka almost spitting out her water.

'Carry on,' Darinka urged.

'So, you have an innate ability, but now you're building on this by learning storytelling skills. When you combine natural talent with skill you develop mastery.'

The church clock chimed the hour. There was a hush as the children had returned to their classrooms.

'Share your spontaneous stories with the children, Darinka. Trust the images that come to you and let the story do the work. You're ready. You already know that if one story doesn't land as you'd like, there's always another one!'

Darinka didn't want to push the intercom button as it would end their conversation. She reached forward to hug Dorothy one last time. When eventually Dorothy stood back and looked at the young woman, they both had tears in their eyes. Darinka's throat was tight. She swallowed hard and moved her hand up towards her lips as tears ran down her cheeks. 'Thank you,' she gasped between tears. 'Thank you so much.'

Dorothy looking straight into Darinka's eyes, smiling. 'Sharing a story is like planting a seed. Your job is to plant the seed, but then to trust that universal forces – mightier beings – will take care of the growing.'

Darinka put her hand in her pocket and discovered the little hanky Dorothy had given her the very first time they'd met, at the windmill. She had washed it, meaning to give it back but had forgotten all about it until now. 'Oh, this is yours,' Darinka said, smiling as she held it towards the Wise Woman.

'I'd like you to keep it. When you use it, think of these seven secrets and remember to share them, so that they can be of benefit to others.' Dorothy touched Darinka's face gently, brushing away one of her tears. 'Go well my friend. You are a wonderful mother and a fabulous human being.'

Darinka laughed, throwing away the compliment. 'It takes one to know one!'

Before Dorothy turned to leave for the last time, she spoke quietly, 'Darinka, never be afraid to fail. For what might appear to you to be a catastrophe could well turn out to be a mighty gift, not only for you but for others too.'

As Darinka pushed the buzzer, the gate clicked open. She walked slowly across the car park back to school, clutching the small hanky with its pink heart in one corner. It felt comforting.

STORY GAMES FROM CHAPTER 7

The Story Pot – see page 180
For three or more players

In groups of three to five players ask each individual group to agree on:

1. A girl's name beginning with a letter of the alphabet that you decide: e.g. G. Once they have decided within their own group, ask them to call out their choice. If more than one group has chosen the same name this word is not added to the Story Pot. Any name which is unique to the group is added to the Story Pot.

2. Next ask them to choose a boy's name beginning with a letter of the alphabet e.g. D. You repeat the same process as above. There are two more rounds, as follows:

3. An object beginning with another letter of the alphabet.

4. A place beginning with a letter of the alphabet.

All the unique words are now in your four Story Pots – one of each of the categories above.

- Ask someone to draw out a word from each Pot for the teller to use to make up a story.
- Alternatively use these words as per the Disrupter in Chapter Six.

Sharing Rhymes in two or more Languages – see page 187

- Share a rhyme in English (or your native tongue) with simple and clear gestures. Repeat it twice or three times. Now share the same rhyme in another language, using the same gestures as above, repeat this once or twice.

- If you use the same rhymes regularly, for example at the beginning or end of your story session, the listeners will share the gestures with you whilst picking up the words from both versions.

Here is a rhyme by Christian Morgensterne, translated from the German:

> *Earth who has brought us this*
> *Sun who has ripened it*
> *Dear sun, dear earth*
> *May you never be forgotten*

> *Erde, die uns dies gebracht*
> *Sonne die es reif gemacht*
> *Liebe Sonne, liebe Erde*
> *Euer nie vergessen werde*

Did you know?

- We tend to judge the confidence of others by their behaviours whilst we judge our own by how we feel. In this way we are biased in how we interpret other people's confidence.

- In 'How to build confidence' by Amy Gallo (Harvard Business Review, 2011) she recommends, 'Be honest with yourself about what you know and what you still need to learn. Practice doing the things you are unsure about. Embrace new opportunities to prove you can do difficult things.'

Further reading...

The Storyteller's Way: Sourcebook for inspired storytelling, by Ashley Ramsden and Sue Hollingsworth.

Game On: Ice breakers, memory games, wordplay and everything in between, by Marley Byng.

'How to build confidence', by Amy Gallo.

This Little Puffin: A treasury of nursery rhymes, songs and games, edited by Elizabeth Matterson.

'Confidence: What Does It Do?' by Richard Petty (watch on YouTube)

Seven Years On

'Time is the wisest counselor of all.'
Pericles

Darinka

Worked in the children's school for two years, during which time she attended several storytelling courses. She supported Rachel to set up an adult storytelling circle in their village and continued to share stories, daily, with her children. She returned to education to study for a Masters in Educational Psychology at Leeds University.

Adam and she still have their arguments but they enjoy being together, alone and as a family. They regularly take the children to Slovenia to visit *Babica* and Darinka's extended family.

She often wishes that Dorothy was available to give her advice about teenagers.

She still has her little hanky with the pink heart.

Adam

Spent over five years working on the three warehouse conversions, which have transformed the canal path into a bustling hive of activity. Two years ago, Adam and

Darinka found a ¾ acre plot of land on which to build their dream home. They sold their terraced cottage and moved into rented accommodation in order to buy it. Planning permission took over 18 months, but Adam hopes to start laying the foundations soon. The family spends many weekends onsite, clearing the land, playing games, sharing picnics, campfires and stories.

Adam went regularly to see a therapist for over three years, which significantly improved his communication skills and his ability to regulate his emotions. He still loves cloud watching.

Tommy
Likes to hang out on the village green with his mates at the weekend – cycling, playing football or cricket. He would rather live in the city and takes the bus into Leeds when his mum lets him. He's not particularly interested in school, although he loves reading comics and graphic novels. After school he takes himself off to Adam's workshop in the village where he is teaching himself how to work in metal and wood. He hates it when his dad gives him too many instructions.

He wishes he were still young enough to go to play on the straw bales at Mrs Oddie's Farm. Sometimes, when no one is looking, he still sucks his thumb.

Marija
Is feisty, dynamic and straight talking. She really enjoys helping her dad on their plot of land whenever she can. She persuaded him to build her a tree platform where she can often be found, lying on her belly listening to music. She prefers non-fiction to fiction and is

currently researching her mum's family tree. Currently she says she wants to study Criminology at university. She is bilingual.

She doesn't really remember Dorothy but likes to lead the family in 'Dotty story Games'.

Luka
Enjoys baking and particularly loves decorating cakes, so he's now in charge of all the family birthday cakes. He is a chatterbox and is popular at school, especially with the girls. He loves nothing better than curling up on the sofa with a bowl of popcorn, watching the TV. His favourite programmes are cookery programmes, and he has plans to write his own cookery book. Luka is bilingual. He has completely stopped hitting and biting!

Nala the Cat
Is 12 years old. She still loves to lie in front of the fire. She likes it even more when Luka is watching TV so she can curl up on his knee.

Si
Has his own plumbing firm, with four employees and spends most of his time at work. After Tess nagged him for a couple of years, he joined an online dating site.

Recently he met Jeya, a widow with three teenage children. They've been on five dates. He is nervous to introduce her to Joe, but for the first time since Shubu died he can see himself being with someone again.

Tess
Achieved good grades in her three A levels, passed her

driving test and went straight to university. Halfway through the second term she dropped out and went travelling. She spent three months working in Nigeria, where some of her mum's family still live.

She now works as an HCA, in the sexual health clinic, at Bradford Royal Infirmary. Her long-term goal is to work for one of the leading African health charities and potentially emigrate to Nigeria.

She misses her mum but it helps to share stories about her with Darinka.

Joe

Is still very quiet. He is studying for his A levels. He fights a lot with his dad and doesn't get on particularly well with Tess. He wants to be an engineer and can't wait to leave school and leave home.

Rachel

Is still married to David. She continues to learn as much as she can about autism and ADHD, particularly in girls.

Having seen how much stories benefited her daughter she began to learn the art of storytelling, including using finger puppets as part of her stories. Schools and libraries in the area often ask her to deliver storytelling sessions, which she can fit around looking after Lucy, who is her main priority.

The adult storytelling club she set up, with Darinka's help, is thriving. They meet monthly and have around 20 regular attendees. She occasionally invites professional storytellers from around the county to be a special guest. She enjoys hearing their different stories and their varying styles.

Lucy
Was eventually diagnosed with autism. She is bright and intelligent but struggles in school, particularly with anxiety. She hides it from most people, except those closest to her. She has certain interests about which she knows everything. She has read the extended Percy Jackson series at least four times. She writes poetry and wants to be an actor. She has a special puppet called Snow who comes everywhere with her. When she was nine years old she told her mum, 'If I can't be a teacher I want to be a Dotty'.

Dorothy
Is sharing storytelling secrets with families who need her. She often thinks about the Dale family and wonders how each of them is getting on.

Is Dorothy real, a fairy-tale godmother or our combined ancestral wisdom? Does she exist inside each one of us, if only we could pause and listen?

As parents I believe we often underestimate our own good sense and judgment. We flounder, wondering what is best for our children until our opinions and decisions are affirmed by an 'expert'. In this book Dorothy acts as the 'expert' to enable Adam and Darinka to grow and improve as individuals and as parents, but also to help them to believe in their own abilities and those of their children.

The Windmill
Remains boarded up, for now...

Acknowledgements

I feel extraordinarily blessed to have met so many wise women and men who have inspired me to be a braver human being and thereby, over time, a better storyteller.

Particular thanks to Dorothy Mary Kathleen, my paternal grandmother, who shared her passion for nature, her memories, her homemade soup and ginger biscuits and most importantly her time and her love.

Thank you to my darling mum for her tenacity, honesty and love of beauty. I am so grateful that we grow closer each and every year.

With gratitude to Tessabella Lovemore who has taught me more than she will ever know, and to Juliana Freeman who is a constant guide and true friend.

Thank you, dad, David Lodge, for igniting my curiosity, for telling me stories, for sharing your family history and for leading the charge to ensure the full restoration of Holgate windmill in York.

Roi Gal-Or, a master storyteller and trainer, for generously sharing so much with me, not least many fantastic story games, and to Alexander Mackenzie, a generous and effervescent teacher, who first introduced me to the magical world of spontaneous storytelling.

I am so grateful to Michael Morpurgo for trusting me with his stories and for believing in me when I needed it most.

Thank you to the many hundreds of children, teachers, librarians, parents and grandparents from whom I have learnt so much.

I'd like to thank everyone who helped me during the research for this book including my dear, inspiring friend

Shirlie Roden, whose love of Slovenia is infectious and to her friend, Nataša Kogoj for sharing her knowledge with me.

I am grateful to Lara Kuppers, Chris Mason, Amanthi Harris and Fi Macpherson for allowing me to share these secrets with them during my research, week by week, and for their invaluable feedback after they'd tested my ideas on their families.

To Susan Rourke and Liz McDougal for their perceptive and thoughtful feedback on my manuscript.

Many thanks to Steph Pyne for providing us with your graphic design talent and skill.

I'd like to thank the extended Wilson tribe for listening to my tales and watching my shows.

To Will and Henry Standing for being so wonderfully enthusiastic about all my stories and story games.

Huge thanks to Sue Hollingsworth, my wise and wonderful friend, an inspiring storyteller and trainer.

Many thanks also to Helen Hart, Phil Perry, Abi Sparrow, Melanie Hawkes Hodge and Miranda Quinney for their kindness, generosity and invaluable counsel.

I am so grateful to Arts Council England. I was afforded the time to write this book as a result of their Develop Your Creative Practice Grant.

I am indebted to 'The Collie Club' without whom I would have missed many of my deadlines.

With much gratitude to Lesley Hart from Author's Pen who held my hand during a crucial part of this process.

To Martin Large, Claire Percival and all the team at Hawthorn Press, for believing in my work and for sharing this adventure with me.

My deepest thanks go to Nicole Keighley, my general manager, who walks by my side, always seeming to know what to do, when, where, why and how at times when I am confused or uncertain.

Thank you, dear Kate Bunce, illustrator of this book, for your perception, joy and immense talent, I love working with you.

I'm blessed to have Paul Wilson standing by my side, bringing so much laughter and creativity into my life.

To darling Sofie, my wise and astute daughter, for lending me your ear and offering your invaluable advice on too many occasions to mention.

Finally, my endless and deep appreciation to John Miller – JJtBW – who sadly is not here to read this book, but whose love and confidence in me has given me the courage to share these secrets with you.

About the Author

As a storyteller, award-winning solo performer, writer and trainer Danyah has been sharing oral stories professionally for over 25 years. She trained in drama, dance and English at Bretton Hall College and later studied at Lecoq in Paris.

Danyah has starred in five theatrical solo storytelling shows, three of which are award-winning, including *I Believe in Unicorns*, by Michael Morpurgo, seen by over 100,000 people including three West End seasons. Oberon Books published the script of this play, co-written with director, Dani Parr.

For two years Danyah was the regular storyteller on BBC Three Counties Radio. She has adapted and recorded Frances Hodgson Burnett's *The Secret Garden* as part of a unique *Story in a Box* experience.

As a storytelling trainer Danyah works nationally in a range of educational settings, libraries, venues, festivals and online. She was a workshop leader at The International School of Storytelling for over 10 years.

Danyah co-produced three mid-scale musicals including Olivier-nominated *Soul Sister – the life and times of Ike and Tina Turner*, co-written and co-directed by John Miller.

Coming soon: A theatrical solo show based on spontaneous storytelling by the same creative team as *I Believe in Unicorns* and the next book in this series – *Seven Secrets of Seasonal Storytelling*.

Follow me:
www.danyahmillerstoryteller.co.uk
Facebook & YouTube: danyahmillerstoryteller
Twitter & Instagram: danyahmiller

www.danyahmillerstoryteller.co.uk to subscribe to newsletters and events.

Bibliography and Resources

Whilst considering what additional reading to recommend to you I realised that, as a neurodiverse person, reading has always been a challenge for me. As a result, most of my learning has come from the oral traditions. I have not personally read all of these books, however they have either been recommended to me by people that I trust and respect or been written by esteemed colleagues. By contrast, the websites below link you to some of the incredible people with whom I've worked in one way or another.

Baric, Maija (2007), *Puppet Theatre,* Hawthorn Press, Stroud

Biddulph, Steve (1998), *Raising Boys: Why boys are different and how to help them become happy and well-balanced men,* Thorsons, London

Biddulph, Steve (2013), *Raising Girls: Helping your daughter to grow up wise, warm and strong,* Harper Thorsons, London

Byng, Marley (2021), *Game On: Ice breakers, memory games, wordplay and everything in between,* Hardie Grant Books, London

Cameron, Julia (1994), *The Artist's Way: A course in discovering and recovering your creative self,* Pan Macmillan, London

Didion, Joan (2006), *The Year of Magical Thinking,* Harper Perennial, London

Higashida, Naoki (2014), *The Reason I Jump: One boy's voice from the silence of autism,* Sceptre, London

Johnstone, Keith (1999), *Impro for Storytellers,* Faber & Faber, London

Kaufman, Scott Barry and Gregoire, Carolyn (2016), *Wired to Create: Unraveling the mysteries of the creative mind,* Tarcherperigee, New York

Leschziner, Dr Guy (2022), *The Man Who Tasted Words: Inside the strange and startling world of our senses,* Simon & Schuster UK, London

Matterson, Elizabeth (ed.) (1991), *This Little Puffin: A treasury of nursery rhymes, songs and games,* Puffin Books, London

Mellon, Nancy (2003), *Storytelling and the Art of Imagination,* Yellow Moon Press, Massachusetts

Morpurgo, Michael (2005), *I Believe in Unicorns,* Walker Books, London

Payne, Kim John (1998), *Games Children Play: How games and sport help children develop,* Hawthorn Press, Stroud

Perrow, Susan (2008), *Healing Stories for Challenging Behaviour,* Hawthorn Press, Stroud

Porter, Max (2015), *Grief Is the Thing with Feathers,* Faber & Faber, London

Ramsden, Ashley & Hollingsworth, Sue (2013), *The Story-teller's Way: Sourcebook for inspired storytelling,* Hawthorn Press, Stroud

Rosen, Michael (2011) *Sad Book,* Walker Books, London.

Samuel, Julia (2017), *Grief Works: Stories of life, death and surviving,* Penguin Life, London

Smale, Holly (2013), *Geek Girl,* HarperCollins Children's Books, London

Spolin, Viola (1986), *Theater Games for the Classroom: A teacher's handbook,* Northwestern University Press, Illinois

Online Articles and Talks

Gallo, Amy (2011), 'How to build confidence', Harvard Business Review.
https://hbr.org/2011/04/how-to-build-confidence

Petty, Richard, 'Confidence: What Does It Do?' TEDx, Ohio State University

Oakenshield, Ollie, 'Imagination, Storytelling and the Importance of Wonder', TEDx, Truro

Zaman, Syeda Sazia and Khanom, Ferdousi (2021), 'What is free play and why should you encourage it at home?', Unicef.org

Websites

Roi Gal-Or

https://www.roigalor.com/

Roi is an internationally acclaimed performing storyteller and workshop leader. For 20 years, he has taught the art and craft of the storyteller to thousands of people around the world. He is co-founder of the International School of Storytelling.

Sue Hollingsworth

https://www.centreforbiographicalstorytelling.com/

Sue has been a professional storyteller, workshop facilitator and leader and coach for over 20 years. Before she founded the Centre for Biographical Storytelling in 2017 she co-founded the International School of Storytelling and Storytelling in Organisations, which pioneered business storytelling in Europe from 1997.

The Foundation for Active Practical Love

https://www.activepracticallove.com

Founded by Tessabella Lovemore who taught in Rudolf Steiner Waldorf schools for 20 years. Since 1994 her work as an education consultant, counsellor and social scientist has concentrated on ways of improving and overcoming problems relating to behaviour, conflict, learning, parenting trauma and relationships.

Alexander Mackenzie

https://www.alexandermackenzie.net

Alexander Mackenzie is an artist, illustrator and storyteller based in Edinburgh. His acclaimed book Humbert Bear, inspired by and dedicated to children with life limiting illnesses, has been translated into seven languages.

Paul Matthews

https://paulmatthewspoetry.co.uk

Paul Matthews is a published poet, internationally acclaimed both for his poetry readings and for the joyful and interactive workshops in Creative Writing that he offers.

The Story Museum

https://www.storymuseum.org.uk/

The Story Museum is a most unusual Museum. It was created to highlight the human need for stories and to celebrate the many ways that people can benefit from them. Their magical spaces and inspiring programme of activities enrich lives, especially young lives, through stories.

The School of Storytelling

https://www.schoolofstorytelling.com/

The School of Storytelling is the longest running storytelling centre of its kind. They have run courses since 1994, welcoming people from all cultures, backgrounds, genders, ages and experience.

Society for Storytelling

https://www.sfs.org.uk/

The Society for Storytelling was founded in 1993 to support and promote storytelling in England and Wales. They provide a central place to find out about storytelling emanating from the ancient art of oratory storytelling.

Praise for *Seven Secrets of Spontaneous Storytelling*

Look for who is the most appreciated person at the dining table, in the pub, in the car on a long drive – it's the one who tells good stories! Danyah makes her living doing it – and she generously gives her secrets away. Anyone at all – mum, dad, someone struggling with shyness – can get better at making others smile, laugh and come alive. It's a form of love.

Steve Biddulph AM. World-renowned author, activist and psychologist

Full of brilliant inspiration, wisdom and practical storytelling tools. I would encourage any carer, parent or teacher (or anyone really...) who wants to connect deeply with the children they are fortunate to spend time with, to read this book. Told in the form of an engaging tale, by such a brilliant storyteller, the power of stories and story-making as a means for social change and personal development, are woven in beautifully and could not be clearer.

Karen Napier MBE. CEO *The Reading Agency*

Like me, you'll probably read the book in one sitting and immediately start playing these delightful storytelling games with the children in your life. Develops the skills and confidence for all the family to enjoy spontaneous storytelling and guaranteed to inspire, educate and transform your relationship to the world of the imagination.

Sue Hollingsworth, storyteller and author of *The Storyteller's Way*

This book is truly inspirational and will give parents the confidence to unleash their imaginations to use stories with their children and have lots of fun. The stories can help parents navigate the normal tricky situations all families face with creativity and humour. The story games at the end of every chapter are full of brilliant ideas to help you get started as a storyteller.

Caroline Penney, author of *The Parenting Toolkit: simple steps to happy and confident children*

More books by Hawthorn Press

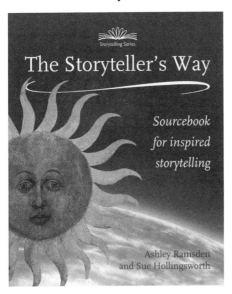

The Storyteller's Way
Sourcebook for inspired storytelling
Ashley Ramsden & Sue Hollingsworth

Everyone can tell a story, but to tell it well you need a certain set of skills. Whether you're starting out or want to develop your storytelling expertise, this book is an essential guide.

The Storyteller's Way contains a wealth of stories, exercises, questions, tips and insights to guide your storytelling path, offering time-tested and trusted ways to improve your skills, overcome blocks and become a confident and inspirational storyteller.

256pp; 228 x 186mm; paperback; ISBN: 978-1-907359-19-4

Storytelling with Children
Nancy Mellon

Telling stories is a peaceful, magical way of creating special
occasions with children. Nancy believes every parent can,
and should, become a confident, creative storyteller,
and that stories told by a parent are a gift to your child,
a wonderful act of sharing and communicating. Nancy's
gentle, practical advice is illustrated with many beautiful,
funny and wise stories created by families who have
discovered how the power of story transforms lives and
relationships.

192pp; 216 × 138mm; paperback; ISBN: 978-1-907359-26-2

The Natural Storyteller
Wildlife Tales for Telling
Georgiana Keable

Here is a handbook for the natural storyteller, with story maps, brain-teasing riddles, story skeletons and adventures to make a tale your own. Adventures between birds, animals and people. Fairytales from the forest and true tales of sea, earth and sky. Georgiana Keable shows through a range of techniques – sometimes the power of the story alone – how to interpret, re-tell and pass these stories on for the future. This diverse collection of stories will nurture active literacy skills and help form an essential bond with nature.

272pp; 228 x 186mm; paperback; ISBN: 978-1-907359-80-4

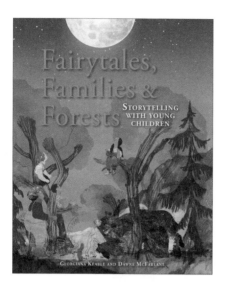

Fairytales, Families & Forests
Storytelling with Young Children
Georgiana Keable and Dawne Mc Farlane

Fairytales, Families and Forests encourages parents and teachers of very young children to tell stories in their family or pre-school. There is a chapter for each year of the child's life from birth to seven years, with age specific stories, verses, games and how to use them, including the use of sign language and special needs.

264pp; 228 x 186mm; paperback; ISBN: 978-1-912480-38-8

Ordering Books
If you have difficulties ordering Hawthorn Press books from a bookshop, you can order direct from our website **www.hawthornpress.com,** or from our UK distributor: BookSource, 50 Cambuslang Road, Glasgow, G32 8NB Tel: (0845) 370 0067, Email: orders@booksource.net. Details of our overseas distributors can be found on our website.

Hawthorn Press